Heartbreak Benediction

Heartbreak Benediction
© 2025 by Brianna Mercedes Scully

For permissions, contact:
Brianna Scully

Cover design by Brianna Scully
Printed in the United States of America

ISBN: 979-8-9994665-0-1

First Edition

For

Humans with their hearts broken open

For

All of my teachers

For

God

Benediction

/ˌbenəˈdikSH(ə)n/

Noun

The uttering or bestowing of a *blessing*, traditionally at the *end* of a religious service.

A benediction is a blessing — either a formal one that you might hear in a church service or an informal one that you might invoke *when you take any leap of faith.*

The noun benediction comes from the Latin roots bene, meaning "well," and diction meaning, "to speak" — literally *to speak well of.*

Once I let myself embrace the darkness fully, the hand of the divine reached out to me. An echoing voice in what felt like an endless void led me back to the light, back to myself. I began to take up space in this life.

Contents

Introduction

I was sitting at my desk choking on my agony. A charged wire whipping around erratically. Sitting very, very still.

I picked up a pen and I wrote a line that kept running through my head. I wrote it around the edges of a square paper — one I'd intended to use for origami and never did. In that moment, and the couple of weeks without him that followed, I felt a faint remembrance of what it was like to be free. What it felt like to be me.

I'd written poems before, I'm sure, but this was different. This was a voice I couldn't hear clearly before — my own, and something greater. A rebellious love that told me these words were not only worthy of being written down but absolutely necessary. If only for my own healing.

I always felt a connection to God, even as I went through the very natural phase of extreme discontent with the oppressive rules some organized religions put in place to control populations. Naturally, I think that is totally separate from what God would have wanted. I believe the divine celebrates our individual and collective liberation. Encourages a persistent call to unconditional love.

In college, I studied cultural anthropology, and I was enraptured by the way religion has always been a human need, not a want — a common thread that allows human civilization to thrive. A favorite concept of mine was Victor Turner's, *communitas*. You know that euphoric feeling at a concert or baseball game? That's what communitas is, a community high on shared devotion. You could call it awe, collective ecstasy, God.

At that time, I also studied Buddhism, Tantra, Mythology, and various esoteric religions. I challenged my beliefs, letting each one open my mind and reveal where my boundaries lay when it comes to the unorthodox. It was in these years that I first heard the phrase "God breaks your heart again and again until it stays open," a quote from Sufi master Hazrat Inayat Khan. I thought then that I was sufficiently heartbroken after dealing with toxic hookup culture and graduating with no friends. I've only ever loved deeply, and mourned fully — I've never had a heartbreak I didn't think perhaps I would never recover from. It was not until I would find resolute assuredness in my own innate self-worth, that returning to love with an open heart would become easeful. Opening more and more to love is a lifelong journey.

I spent much of my 20s in a high-control relationship. I also assumed, for my own self-preservation, that anyone else I may encounter, even platonically, would break my heart. This contributed to keeping my world small; I was playing my part in my own captivity, codependency, unhappiness and perpetual state of heartbreak. The same kind of existential heartbreak I still feel to some extent daily when I pray for all those suffering around the world in ways big and small.

After I moved back to New York in 2018, I felt called to go to church, but for whatever reason, I couldn't make it a priority. I wasn't raised particularly religious, but I found myself making bargains — calling in desired outcomes I thought would bring me peace and happiness. "God, please let his business lawsuit work out in his favor, then he will treat me better. If it does, I will return to your house." I heard a response back to these first prayers and promises, but the responses didn't suit my pursuit of a future with him, so I shook them off as anxiety and thoughts from my ego, not messages. I confess, in my experience, it takes a while to learn to differentiate those threads.

I continued to set aside parts of myself, as loving him and contorting to his preferences took all of my shrinking capacity. In the whispers of "this is not what love should feel like," the subtext was "this is not what your life feels like; you are not meant to hide." I broke up with him in the end, simply listening to my body and this voice coming from within. There was something, and I didn't know what, that was much bigger that I had to do. I still am not sure I know exactly what that is, but I promised myself I would go after it. I would allow myself to start taking up space.

I went through a deeply challenging breakup, the kind that rips your soul to shreds, the kind of extracting of your soul from theirs that leaves a lot of pieces missing. This was the kind of breakup that is less of a breakup and more of a prolonged exorcism, and you keep getting possessed. You're a possession remembering how to be a person. It took two years from the moment I felt the knowing that it was over to when it could finally, truly, be over.

Typically, when someone refers to being heartbroken, you imagine a sudden dumping. Well, it comes in all shapes and sizes, but they all yield grief. The beauty of that fact being that it can inch you towards crucial conversations with God. For me, deciding to end my relationship once and for all broke my heart. It took so much courage, and I couldn't even do it face to face. The times I'd tried in person, the part of me that loved him more than I could reason would see his pain and immediately hold him close. The part of me that reflexively bent to him would fawn and freeze in self-preservation. So, the cowardly approach became my bravest act. His making me promise I'd never reach out to him again became his greatest gift to me. My choosing to be the soul I was brought here to be became the first of many leaps of faith.

I believe in unconditional love, but relationships are highly conditional. I don't want any woman, or person for that matter, to

13

live their life totally shut down — sacrificing themselves on another's altar. I am against living life as a sidekick, making yourself small and easily digestible. It's a cliché for a reason: you have to choose yourself; you have to believe you deserve more and are worthy of it. I know that you can know it, read it, and be told it, but it will all seem like idealistic platitudes until you allow yourself to really hear the whispers — the ones coming from within.

At some level my entire spiritual journey can be distilled down to first hearing the inner voice, then having the courage to listen to the inner voice, and finally distinguishing the divine knowing from the anxious dialogue my ego creates to keep me safe in the familiar. Once I could hear the symphony of life's collective brilliance, I was able to slowly add my own note — my unique frequency — and play my part; I recognized this was God. This was the goddess within me. This was the great miracle and mystery that brought me here.

Beginning in 2021, I finally started going church. I've told a number of people about my hobby of what I've jokingly called "church tourism." I went to a different church service each Sunday — primarily Episcopalian, Catholic, and non-denominational, with a few others sprinkled in. There are thousands of churches in NYC — 2,000 physical church buildings and at least three times as many that meet in other spaces. It's safe to say that of all the ones I have visited, I haven't even scratched the surface, especially since many I went to more than once due to geographical convenience. I knew it didn't matter to me what denomination I visited, but I wanted to know how the different rituals and services were conducted, what kind of music was played, if any, how the Eucharist was performed, and what message the sermon had for me that day. The point of this was not to make a statement. It was a solo and personal mission. I wanted to connect with God, to get closer to that feeling that brought me such solace. I wanted to let my eyes well with tears from this new emotion. To feel that it was possible to have hope for a better future, to know that I could dream again.

In being with that divine love, being in love, in relationship with love, relationships took on a new meaning for me entirely. All humans desperately need to be loved and are equally deserving of it. The ways we separate ourselves from each other, and ultimately from our true selves, is a strange, learned compulsion — a torture we are rewarded for as a society. I believe that love is the greatest sacred force, which can deeply connect two people and weave their souls in a gorgeously ineffable way, but healing must first be recognized within yourself. All relationships begin with the one you have with yourself.

To be loved by another, the ending to the fairytales little girls grow up with, is just a part of the love this world offers. When devout people speak to their relationship with God, "Jesus first" etc., I used to cringe, sometimes I still do. However, for those who really mean it, I've come to realize that their own internal experience of divine love comes first. To truly love yourself is to find that source of sacred love within you. No healer can fix you until you really allow yourself to realize that it comes from you. Romantic love is beautiful, but there are deeper loves — love of a child, your relationship with God, the sacredness of this world, and your existence in it.

What I've learned is that all beings I pray to, Jesus, Mary Magdalene, Archangel Michael, Mother Earth, Lakshmi, and Kali, to name a few, are always accessible to me. I can be in relationship with their unique frequencies and insights. I don't feel it is contradictory to pray to Mother Mary and Saraswati in the same breath. I learned through my devotion that the only way to really connect with a higher power is to search within yourself. God speaks to you through your body; that is how you alchemize any circumstance to live all the way alive.

There is something to be said about transcendence, but being fully present in your body, in your lived experience, in your expression, is the real good stuff.

You have to be a witness to your own divinity, to literally feel it moving through your body. You also must seek it with and in others — feel the communitas. I grew up as a dancer, it was a huge part of my identity. I discovered, in unraveling my truth by listening to my physical body, just how important dance was to me. When I am processing something, I must move with it. On the other side of dancing with the emotion I often write a poem. Our bodies hold all of our experiences, especially ones our minds cannot, they are portals to our subconscious. The way we move with our feelings and sensations can transmute them and help us heal. A broken heart was the catalyst for me waking up to that truth. I know I am not alone in that experience.

The memory of a magical photoshoot I did in a lake in 2021, reminds me of the importance of witnessing. It was early on in this journey, and I was holding back. A retreat leader placed an invitation before me: "Would you like to scream?" I timidly said yes; she said, "Scream it." I screamed YES on repeat at the top of my lungs. I said yes to that experience, to life, to myself. I remember feeling like I was back in my body for the first time in a long time — a wild realization for someone who has had a lifelong love of movement. It would take a long time for me to be able to sustain being in that embodied state. That night, the last night of this retreat, I was vivacious, bright, and warm. To be given permission to not hold back is a gift, to be seen in your full self, not only your sorrow, but all of it, from your anger to your fullest joy, your awkwardness and your sexuality. Not being rejected starts with not rejecting any parts of yourself. There is nothing holier than to be whole.

Creative practice is how many of us connect to spirit — as many different texts describe. In my experience, it is true that once I am embodied and have connected with that spark of aliveness flowing through me, I can create. I can be creative because I am not in survival mode. These poems did not come from my mind but through my body.

This book is a collection of moments and emotions from my journey back to myself — my reclamation of all that is me without shame or apology. Also, with shame and apology. It involved picking up all parts of myself that I'd exiled over the course of my life to fit in or keep the peace; releasing through my body to make space as I built up my capacity to be her; embodying this being, and in time realizing the process was devout all along. To honor oneself is a prayer.

Since I was diagnosed with ADHD as a child, I have always tried to not overidentify with diagnoses or labels. Yet, for context, it is worth noting that a number of therapists and coaches tried to convince me that my ex was a narcissist or a covert narcissist. I kept trying to find a different professional, who would give me different advice, who would not tell me to leave him — but I knew they were right. I don't think this makes him a bad person, but certainly not a safe partner. I also know it resulted in my needing to recover from complex post-traumatic stress disorder (CPTSD). It was a slow and looping process that required a lot of support after having walked on eggshells for years. It involved writing a lot of poems.

Everything that I've experienced in this life that has totally broken my heart has been my greatest teacher. Every grief cracks me open as if to prove that my capacity for love can grow. I've come to learn that the darkness we carry is our assignment, a divine blessing to experience being with and learning from. The deeper you can grieve or touch pain, the more joy you will be able to access. The heaviness you fear, the weight that drags you down into the underworld, is trying to heal you — if you allow yourself to feel it all the way. I have never experienced anything more joyful than realizing, after sitting with the pain, that it cracked my heart open into an ever-bleeding portal for God to fill and flow into.

Sometimes when you don't know how to describe an experience, all you can do is write poems about it. When I started writing, I was so twisted up. I was behaving much like an addict, but to the relational dynamic. The thing about trauma is that it's hard to really put the experience into words. Especially when the experience is wrapped in real, crazy, passionate love. It's the most confusing knot and ping pong tournament inside you. You must titrate your healing with a lot of grace. Editing this collection down was an agonizing process for me as I demoted or protected, and exposed, pieces of my heart and heartache.

This book is decidedly not about my ex, nor anyone else I've dated over the past few years, all of whom were absolutely invaluable in my healing process. It is about my relationship to love.

This book is about my experience, my hard-fought battle to reclaim myself. My prayer is that it allows someone else to feel a little less alone and to remember they can slowly reclaim their power, no matter how long it takes. You can have reparative experiences and rewire your neural pathways until you are living in a different world. There's a part of me that is ashamed that it took me this long to share my poetry, that it took me this long to compile this book. I've been processing all of the emotions I had inside me, taking several underworld journeys, and slowly categorizing which beliefs were mine and which were not. Part of my devotion to God became devotion to writing regularly and trusting what was coming through.

Allowing myself to actually release these poems has been its own psychedelic trip. These poems were a process of finding my voice, my creativity, owning it, and sharing it. I wrote a poem about how much I love pickled onions. It got cut, and I'm a little sad about it. As I publish this book, I am not the woman who wrote these poems. Still, I love her dearly, and her work deserves to be bravely shared. It was hard to stay focused on completing a phase of my life that I have long been ready to move on from; to claim that my heart is worthy of being shared imperfect and broken open required fighting against all the inhibitions that made me want to crawl back inside my shell never to be seen again — proving that you can expand your window of tolerance by slowly, lovingly, cultivating it, even if it takes years. You can alchemize anxiety into aliveness, shaking awake with every realization that your courage did not kill you — that the integrity of your resilience has made each small personal victory sweeter.

You can alchemize your heartbreak into anything you want.

GRIEF

There is only one thing to do with grief: be with it.

Grief is never momentary, but cyclical — regardless of any effort at soothing, it comes back — just as poignant as last time, and the time before, and the time before. Like the receding shore revealing seaweed and shellfish, it is a reminder to look closely at what is underneath the surface.

Grief about a lost love is difficult to reconcile, because unlike death, you are grieving a living separateness that can be sensed. You can feel their life on the other end of this grief, teasing you. As with loss from death, there is always a reflection of love — a very real love that does not end on the other side of separation.

Grief can be about nothing in particular, and everything all at once. I sometimes grieve for what I cannot control — world events and general chaos, as well as for others. As profound as this grief is, it does not stop me from eating, bathing, or breathing, as personal loss has in my experience. It is the depth of personal experience with devastation that allows us to grieve with genuine empathy and compassion.

Grief, like all human emotions and experiences, is entirely unavoidable. It is our required curriculum; it is part of what we are here for — a byproduct of our complex hearts and inevitable mortality. We have to notice when it knocks for our attention and give it space.

With that space, the mere acknowledgment of it and surrender to it, the cycles become longer, bigger, and wider. Hours, then days, then months, can go by without getting caught in the riptide. Eventually the story of heartbreak will feel far away, and the grief becomes a teacher. You may reach for grief's hand like a fond memory, recognizing it again as simply love.

The Ruins

I didn't think about you
Shapes in the smoke fade to vapor
Months fade to a single picture
Search to place us where it started
Buried beneath the rubble embraced

Gym with a rock wall we never climbed
Rose bushes infested with centipedes
Cards spread across our dining table
Rare jewels we took to our tomb

Time sped up and disappeared entirely
The ruins tell stories of those long gone
Skeletons and artifacts

The Journey

I've been carrying a heavy grief for a long time

I've been so consumed with its weight, and I couldn't keep it in

I needed to find something to do with it

A concoction of love and pain so large there was no container
        I could find it wouldn't spill out of

Making a mess

I left for somewhere I could maybe find joy in the midst of it
Things I enjoy to yield leverage for this burden
        so nothing else gets hurt

I needed to go where no one would bother me
        nor really speak to me at all

I needed to be totally alone with it
        To look clearly

Just let it sit across from me at the dinner table
The breakfast table
For me to consume bite by bite
and try to digest

Let me hold its hand through lunch and walk with me for miles

I needed to be intimately alone with it, like learning what seduces a
new lover

You can try to make sense of each gesture

But there remains an unexplainable chemistry
Intuition, like a reflex
That dictates the moves we make
And the feelings experienced in our bodies

Discovering each tender spot that teeters between pleasure and pain

Exploring new sights and sensations
Chasing that same delectable tingling you get after orgasm
And after the kind of sob that bubbles up from the deepest depths
of your soul

Worth every effort to feel that sense of lightness and release

There I was, alone, shedding
Basking in the vibrating glow of beautiful things in life
That make oceans pool in the lip of your eyes
A vista, a painting, the ending to a story of true love

Veil

Places have a way of snapping you back to a time
You remember, but it feels intangible
Like you weren't really there
But you can still feel the dry mouth, the dry heaves
Taste his breath and feel the yearning
The world in 2D, covered in a thin veil, a sheet of rice paper
The throbbing of pleasure pain
He is the only thing keeping you from floating away
No wonder this space only feels vaguely familiar
Like a room you've seen only in pictures
A life someone read to you in a story once
Not your own

And I'd Do It Again

Amongst so much beauty, my eyes are swelling with sorrow
rather than awe

Running through these rows
as if I could outpace the greatest test I've faced

I want to be with you forever

I want to eject with great force from where being with you pulled me

Healing is cyclical

And I didn't know dipping my toe back in would feel like drowning

The nausea bubbles up and seeps out of my eyes involuntarily,
periodically through my day

Flay my skin and let my blood

Anything to rid my body of this pain

Please pop me like a pimple so the ache goes away
Cut my fingernails too short; nick me with a blade
Stab me in the heart with a fucking knife

I wouldn't know the difference

Besides the fact that I'm choosing this
I chose to feel this way

And I'd do it again

Are You Going to Learn to Trust Yourself?

Breaking your own heart is the hardest part
When you leave, you live with the guilt
An anger that can only be directed at yourself

Therein lies the question and the cure
Are you going to learn to trust yourself?

That your body knows what it's doing
It will bring you back to life
Endure the labor of your rebirthing

Like any initiation, there are no shortcuts
No mentor nor doula can do this work
Carry on kicking and screaming

Even if you can't get out of bed,
Daydream about dying
It's time for an exorcism
Dispel the demons from your lungs
Breathe in new air

Don't question yourself now that you are living
The grip of grief feels grounding
You can drown in the fog if you get too comfortable
The effort is in pulling your head above the mist

Oh, gorgeous, loving heart will remember how
Kiss her forehead, smile, weep
Rock her gently back to sleep

Puzzle

Grappling with each idea
Grasping around the table, eyes darting
Fiddling with each piece, studying the corners and grooves
Holding each part of us with care
Thoughtfully, desperately,
Trying to figure out where you fit into my life

I've found so many of my missing pieces
I assumed you'd make a perfect match, eventually

Drip

I'm somewhere nestled between my future and my past

Healing deep wounds means re-breaking everything that needs to be reset

Every motion forward aches a while

The wind in the trees, my mother's perfume, hot city garbage, that unsettling twinge when you mispluck a guitar

There is so much alive in my heart

I call it joy and weep in its largeness

It whispers, my name is grief, and I understand why joy seems to hurt so much

I'm tired of how much grief has tortured me, but it always comes back to the surface

Not in missing him in the same way, but in grieving all that we were building and who I thought I'd be

Anger at why I stayed, why I left, why I couldn't change him, why I was the problem

Another strum on the mistuned guitar, every nerve in my body

I don't know the right note

I no longer know what to do when my heart aches so badly I feel like I could puke

There is no rationalizing. You're thinked-out
        Tapped

The sap has drained dry
You're feeling a little empty

There is nothing sweet to make sense of this process

Just the aching agony that creeps up as the wounds attempt to heal

Drip, drip

Yours Truly

I've never felt understood

I expect to be misunderstood

I fear connection, and I push people away

Where does that heartbreak end and I begin?

Years into feeling the abject vacancy

From each residency taken up in my life

How is it possible that after everything, a piece of my heart is still yours?

And yours

And yours

And yours

Kink of Losing You

I like poking the wound
I want to look back and remember
Reminisce and weigh the odds in retrospect
Romanticize the brutality of the feeling
The bittersweet, gorish kink of losing you
Experiencing it on repeat
The pain reminds me of us
I catalogue my cinnamon sugar memories
And I feel less alone in missing you
That thread I can follow into my past
Where on the other end my fingers nearly graze your form —
Until I feel you too much and the evidence rises across our skin
Energetically spying on your present
Where I don't belong and chose not to be
At least I'm doing it with love
You hurt so good
I'll always look to you with love

Erase Thought

Shake my brain like an Etch-A-Sketch
The thought of where he may be
When I'm so far from his
Craving attention that belongs to someone new
Sharp breath out
Forward light beam straight ahead
Eyes on the road

What If

Do you think he remembers what my love feels like?
How I used to bathe him in it
I remember the sweet smell of the rain on the pavement
As he held my hand

There is a lot I want to tell him
So much he was right about, and I knew it then too

I hope he woke up terrified by his darkest shadows
So he could finally find the light
So he could really love

I'm still not over it
That's become clear
I'd show him all the scars and how they've healed

Take him on a tour through the gaping hole in my heart
That he left
When I pushed him out of my life

What if I was so curious about the yearning
What if the white noise lullaby of dying didn't ring through my head
What if I was revealing all the beauty and truth I'd promised myself
at the rupture

I have no interest in fitting in

I don't understand how I didn't notice that within the fresh flowers
I'd picked up from the farmers market, an entire world existed
I came home to seeds or excrement decorating my coffee table
I'd left a Mason jar bouquet in the sun
A two-inch caterpillar, thick and munching, stared at me

The inchworm I'd found on my shoulder started to make sense
I'd left him last week on a clover
Weeds growing in a dead plant from my ex, still on my balcony
An island in its small dish filled from the rain
A smaller, thinner caterpillar appeared
I didn't dare search for more
I felt their presence and took the entire jar out the door

I Wrote a Book for You

Hundreds of pages untangling love and grief
Cataloging years of being gutted with heartbreak
I miss you and send you love in a prayer every day
Only not in the way that I once did
When my soul orbited yours like a planet around the sun

It started as a whisper and grew into a roar
The voice inside me that said it was over
The ache in my chest that told me to fight for us
The fire of my soul faded, and one path could rekindle its embers

I couldn't count the tears by the gallon
Overflowing till I ran dry, like a raisin
Still sweet, but shrunken

I wrote a book about him
Dripping with heartache and grief
A love letter through to the final page
Still a profoundly changed woman holds the pen

Fuller than ever
Still weeping as pockets of yearning continue to bubble to the
surface from where they lay
Stuck
Bubbles slowly float to the top of the glass
Sparkling

We never stop loving
We crack further open to make space for more
The real joy of living
Deep pain carves the capacity to hold pleasure

Spiral down to the gooey center
Butterscotch caramel
Sweet sticky stuck
Delightful uncomfortable
Sweet but not safe

Manipulate me harder baby
Question my sanity
You inside me
Criticize me

This book scratches the surface of my soul
Cataloging millions of little deaths endured
Extracting a decision so in opposition with my perception of myself
That it made me physically ill

Staring at a page to express my pain in words
Unable to recount stories even to myself
The thread of cold dissociation lingers in the mist
Smudges and scribbles of formless thought

There was no negotiation
I had signed a contract for who I'd have to be
You helped me grow, and grow I did
Away from you and out of us

The Gift

Even if it rotted and you threw it away
I stay in awe at pressing dried flowers into art
There is sweetness in such luscious life made permanent —
made new in its intentional patient death

The parts of your brain, your heart — daisies and vines
I tried to fix us, fix you, fix me
Rejection and failure
I imagine you gave my art away, and I see it one day
I drop to my knees and sob
The grief that will always live in me
The part of my heart that will always love you

I found another soul, beautiful and tortured
Fresh soil where I could hold my broken pieces
His scars too raw; my soul deeply cracked
The loves we'd lost still stained our sheets
He was careful not to press promises between glass panes
I wanted to make beauty from our deaths to display

Artist longing to love him like a project
Pulled deeper now into the landscape of grief
A seemingly endless field to fall down
To die, rot, grow, bloom

The Middle

I hate you for proving them right and making me hide you
For torturing my knowing and seducing me back
For not being able to step up and love me or yourself
Wide open for you but clenched and bracing
For the inevitable downfall, the mistake I feel myself making

I know they know, and they know I won't tell them
But I'm lying and crying and distant with some new friend

You tell me why I love you; remind me I'm lucky
I bet you don't tell your friends you still fuck me

I cried in surrender, the best feeling I'd ever had
Between us, a tornado in full storm
The rain that came tasted like your manipulations

Love is embarrassing because your whole heart's at risk
They color outside the lines and place you in the oven
Shrink you down hang you as a charm from their hat
Trade all your same memories with the next up at bat

They sway to tiny dancer; you play it for her too
In four years, you'll run out of tricks; what will you do?
It wasn't all that bad; see, I can gaslight me too
Still, I know what love is, and I know I did love you

I'm somewhere in the middle
The revolving door's stuck, and nobody can get in
I much prefer cathedrals with stained glass windows

I go alone, avoiding anyone's opinion
Shattering, refracting
Coloring my life back in

To Sob

All I could do today
Was roll around and sob
Stretch out on the floor to contract and sob
Lean on the wall and sob
Hold myself in it and sob
Feel the agony of getting exactly what I've been asking God for
A push to take the next step and release anything holding me back
Who I need to become to be of service, heal myself and others
Not separately, expressing the tincture of my own grief
Allowing the pain to move through my body
In clumsy, awkward, ugly, rigid ways
Sharp suck in for enough air
To sob

To Have and To Hold

I took all my love, and I slowly built a bed for me to rest
I took each word of loving reassurance and wrote it on my skin
I took my gentle kisses and stretched to reach my knees with my lips

The sensual touch I learned to calm your nervous, shaking breath,
      I now hold myself with
I am the receiver of my alchemical attention
I took all my anguish and arranged it into a bouquet
I gave it water and a container of its own

DISSOCIATION

I am resisting writing this — tapping into this emotion at all invites shutting down and avoiding what I most desire. Take a deep breath with me, the kind where you make a low noise on the exhale. Notice the vibration of your own voice. Breathe presence through your forehead.

Dissociation feels like floating away and, at the same time, being swaddled too tightly in a sheet. The safe space of zoning out and not knowing where you go for hours. It feels like you are wearing a weighted vest you can't take off and like you are totally weightless. It's becoming very small, imperceptible — shrinking into as little space as you can occupy on this Earth.

Dissociation and depression walk hand in hand for me; they are best friends and continuously beget one another. When I am in a reactive trauma spiral, when everything feels too overwhelming, positively or negatively, I tend to totally shut down. Dissociation is a freeze response. Sometimes freeze is subtle, like living on mute or in a black-and-white film. Other times it gets up in my face; I am frozen solid, unable to move or talk. I have to stay there until I begin to shake, like an antelope having just closely escaped a lion, bringing my nervous system back online.

It is important to be cognizant of what you tend towards: freeze, fawn, fight, or flight. We all have these responses a little depending on circumstance, but for me, the big ones are fawning and freezing. Healing from freeze meant moving, slowly, to recollect fragments of myself that had become a collection of shattered objects. It felt like relearning how to be myself. Creating permission to be a little more alive today than I was the day before, non-linearly, of course.

Depression can be scary because, in my experience, it is noticing living in freeze — energetically shut down — but unable to pull yourself out of it. Realizing that your life is on too tight and you can't stretch it or change it; there is a sense of desperation. It's living with trapped emotion, like a too-full balloon that could pop, making basic tasks insurmountable. It's a *shame* that pushes you further into your own fog — to the point where you can't seem to access your feelings — the one thing you need to feel anything or feel better. A sea of depression arises from neglecting one's own feelings. The first step is to notice the little aches in your body, how your knuckles beg to pop, or that pit of despair in your chest.

There are those of us who meet with darkness in the daytime and pray for light to find us. That light will be coming from within you; you gather the matches in each tiny effort to emerge. You begin to see in the dark. You learn how to face building your own fire to be set free.

Good Morning

Depression sneaks in like a sudden breeze, rustling the drapes

The goosebumps rise on my skin, and I'm reminded of the loneliness I chose

Nauseous with emotion, my frozen body won't release its vice grip on the moment

Difficult to move each muscle since my soul has vacated —

Shriveled up to exist as a lump in my throat

She's here again; we've got her; don't move

A never-ending well, so scary to dive down

They don't know how hard it is to do anything at all

Heavy breathing, shallow lungs,

Aching, living with the pain,

Trying to coax a sob in hope of relief

Tell me where grief ends and my life begins

Grit
Courage
Go out for your morning coffee

Seeking Contentment

Piercing loneliness — have you heard of it?
Sitting in the utter stillness that holds my truth
Shaking towards ecstasy to experience my raunchy aliveness

Do you eat your meals all ingredients mixed together?
        Or separate clear portions?
Do I know what it feels like to not be alone?
Did you ever dream of going to New Orleans just to find a tourist
trap?

Maybe in a castle or a field of flowers
Here in a box, totally safe in a dangerous city
Ground meat and rice

Living in lower case letters and hot cups of cocoa
I found myself doodling flowers in the margins of my work
The safer I felt, the deeper my yawns got
Still, I judged myself for sleeping

Fragments

Pinky finger aching, grinding tiny bones
Nerve endings strangle in a cobra's winding grip
Wring me dry; I hang without a drop
Sitting still I shriek in silent moans
Dripping sweat I strip layers in the cathedral
Bursting to tears upon the precipice
Gnawing, unidentifiable emotion
cracks my throat and binds each joint to pop
Eating frozen cherries in a hot bath
Adding salt, but still can't quench my thirst
Filtering my water searching for salvation
My rectangle feeds me my daily Rorschach test
My blood flows blue raspberry jolly rancher
Finding your grace to wash me clean of chaos
Love in and out like oxygen and dreams come true in aligned action
and I'm hungry
I'm shaking in your heat, my knowing
Wipe my hands I bleed on blank pages
Divine chest compression CPR
Screaming, singing, white decor
Gloss my body and fight the door
Metal plates and magnets
Mosaics colors fragments

Where Am I?

Sometimes the world stops making sense
You've retracted the anchor tethering you to reality

When there is nothing to do and nowhere to go,
You can pluck yourself off the track and build momentum into the void
The black hole of infinite mystery, where the task is solely to listen

Today I felt like doing nothing
Took a walk and stared at the wood chips
Old men and beautiful women milled about the garden soaking in the flowers

And I was there

Sipping in hot soup on the first warm day
My inner child asked me really, really nicely
My heart had the capacity to say yes

Linger

Linger a little longer in my heart
Keep my soul alight
Without you, it is dark
I don't want your future
But what is mine?
How do I start?
Seems familiar

Linger beside me, rest until I part
Keep the soft blanket of night at bay
Enough to mark
The passing of time
From when I lay with you
When I last played with you
Finally, away from you

Linger fingers in mine for just one song
Sway my body close to yours; I'm almost gone
Anger wells and my lips turn down to scowl
What's so special about her?
That's feeling foul

Linger with that feeling for a while
Longer still
Maybe forever
Till you smile
Pray to the Goddess, won't you, child
Down on your knees or totally wild

Linger as the sweat rolls down your brow
Catch each salty drop with your tongue
Let out a howl

Make that face where you twist to that place
Where you wring yourself out without a trace of grace

Linger beside me, I am just a child
Hold this hurt — this fear — until my burdens mild
Lay a flannel blanket
Light a soft and flickering fire
And just stay with me

Linger — I know they'll show up this time
What was promised is already mine
Let salt air float in; I'm sitting here still wired
Bathe me in safety
Until I feel inspired

The Myth

I'm not always confident in this myth
My deepest truth or wildest delusion
Oral tradition, each line an elaborate allegory
I may forget the details in my dictation
Flounder in feeling capable of withstanding time
Remember a dream worthwhile
Worth surrendering to with a hum
I tell a tale about a woman
Whose courage conquered all in the end
One lost and broken heart at a time
She served dishes of quiet comfort
Sailed the seas and received messages
In the form of tiny dogs atop a mountain
Coaxing her to realize that she is already home
The myth continues with each step she takes
She only needs to grasp it
A thread pulling her tall to the sky
The puppeteer and the puppet
God within and without
She followed the impulse with the discomfort
Not knowing the destination or who was really in control
Trust is the power that translates her fable
Brings any meaning at all to the table

Liminal Space

With each passing day, I remain
In the liminal space
Where a woman with a bruised and bloodied heart
Aches to belong to something greater than herself —
Something greater than what's expected of her to survive

I'm not where I was, but I'm still floating
Still knee deep in this place
I trace the lines of my body
Sketch my wandering attention
To make a map of myself

Here, in this right now
And I'm wondering somehow
Will I make this time worth it?
Or am I just waiting for you?

Here, pacing until the doors open
And my heart lets him in
Takes on my religion
Inspires sin

A destination where I feel at rest
Tell me, how long until I'm at my best?

I'll talk about my dreams for hours
Hide in my room of half-baked ideas
And I'll spread myself like butter and jam
Across the floor, where my life began

And I'm just wondering right now
Why autonomy feels like a burden

This transition was supposed to be mine
I just thought maybe it would be fine
To be alone for a time
I'm free
But where's serenity?

The answer can't be with just me
May the aches and impulses,
The flowers and the forces
Somehow show me the way

Callihan

Our child cried out to me in a dream, Callihan

I gave him to you along with my other hopes for our life together
Right from my womb to the room I find myself in
Mourning his absence
He cried for his mother to hold him, Callihan

The sound brought clarity to the decisions
        that kept me hidden from purpose
It was out of my hands, Callihan
With a mother's wrath I will fight for you back

In the dimension where you exist, and I'm there loving you madly
I'll take a stand, Callihan
Reconcile with whatever demon made me abandon you

In whatever land
Know I love you and will protect you if I can, Callihan
If you are him, the part I saw hurting, I am there too

In any lifetime, I am here loving you
Come whatever lesson resides in that piece of my heart
Estranged or devoted to you, Callihan

Gold Chains

Balances my contradictions, my pain, my pleasure
Fills my home with sweetness, flowers, and pastels
Brings me to spaces I can fill with my love

Write down all your little thoughts
Collect them like treasured jewels
Hide them at the end of the rainbow

The shackles that bind me melt into gold
Dripping —
Leaving bangles

Holding the remembrance, my ancestors
The fear that keeps me safe
A rose blooms in the ashes where I stood
I placed myself in a dark abandoned lot
A garden to die to heal to grow

Untangling knots in my delicate heart
Chainmail made of gold won't stop me from bleeding
When my heart is smeared across my skin
I can't fathom anything but bathing in it

Clarity brings confidence — I'm getting there
Memories, resentments, longings
Tangled up in a forgotten jewelry box
Gold chains seemingly bound together forever
Patience, deep breaths, and love

They will separate

Owl in the Night

I'm under a canopy of linen sheets and tree branches
The night sky filled with stars
A blanket holding us down
Gravity

A welcome sensation when life seems to invite floating away

It may bother the neighbors or itch in your ears
My voice hitting decibels my throat hardly reaches
But my soul requires
A stretching into the heights of ethereal love, it roars

Does it matter where I sit quietly, as long as I can hear you
I'm about to find out, and I imagine myself another level taller
Where I not only squint to see fairies in the grassy fields,
but strain to see you beneath the stucco rooftops you hide under

The way I contemplate the perspective of an atom
The lifestyle of the bacteria in my gut
My experience, the uncontrollable forces of their universe
A decision or indecision; a tidal wave or lighting strike

I sing with owls who howl just out of sight
Hunting in the night, eyes able to focus beyond where I can see
Though I need only change from where I perceive

From the collapse of my breath, to the wind it becomes
Where once lay fear, sit limitations, and those are temporary
I can shift; I can move to see past them

Luteal

Day 21 and the veil drapes over the world
A subtle, bittersweet edge takes rest on small moments
A weight anchors in my bed frame
I may start watching my body from a third person perspective
I'll spend a week or so trying to get back inside
By then, I'll be lightheaded and bleeding
Soon the record will stop skipping
Back to your regularly scheduled programming

Marinate

You can't build healthy habits by punishing yourself
I feel just a little bit like I'm drowning
All the vices, simple tastes I employ today to soak in
It's just a cold or something, but it smells of chlorine
Neither scotch nor shrooms heals it, nor bad TV
Rom-coms or comedy specials
Perhaps the water will drain
If I marinate in this loneliness today

Sweater

Nervous system a well-loved sweater
I think it'll feel better
More satisfying
If I pull

Grit and Grace

I learned I must always belong to myself

As I unravel the threads, I know all the realities, in their unique
cosmic truth, exist at once
Being with you was loving, fulfilling, chaotic, abusive
A playful bounce house
A disguised prison

Productivity looks like crying
Self-compassion is a terrific accomplishment

Biding time, waiting for the tide to go out
Take the dark fog with it
I look for you across the east river and tell myself I'm doing fine
Canceling plans, locked in my apartment
Piercing deep in this fog of lost souls

If I keep moving, maybe I won't be sucked back down
Walking to nowhere
Dancing alone in my 400-square-foot home
Trying, crying, running, shaking
Create more space for joy
Compounding the oxygen my lungs can hold

Resilience and softness coexist inside me
Holding space for grit and grace

I'm no longer trying to make people see me clearly
Choosing to be at peace in a chaotic world
We can only take the next right step

When I think I finally have it figured out and the rain has cleared, it's time to die again, and my newly sprouted flowers fall to become mulch, so I may grow taller

Smiling as children sing, and my nerves spark across my body

Hopscotch steps of sunlight through my retinas

SOFTNESS

We cannot stay clenched indefinitely; eventually, our fist must open so we can begin to receive. As I navigated my own melancholic drama, I began to find pockets of sweet tenderness and humor — the pleasure in lounging naked in a sunbeam, laughing, knowing with my windows wide open, all of New York City could see me lying there if they were to look. The warmth of love was coming from the sun, and I could feel it thawing out the remaining cold armor I'd grown. It could be meaningful, and it could be so simple and innate, all at the same time — mere moments of softness.

So many of us feel like outsiders. Acknowledging how we can comfort ourselves helps us find belonging within ourselves, and with God. From that space, we can go out into the world feeling our inherent worth, even if it's just a little spark: to sit on a park bench and whisper, "I belong here," or take the best seat in the coffee shop; to take the first bite of your meal and really taste all the pleasure in that flavor and nourishment; to smile at the cooing baby and make friends with your local dogs; to tell the flowers your secrets and hum softly as you snuggle into bed; to lovingly care for yourself and look at the world with a healthy dose of sweetness; taking those rose-colored glasses that may have once pulled you into something unhealthy, using them to see yourself with unconditional love, and turning that love towards the world and the spaces you occupy.

Softness is about self-compassion — giving yourself grace and leading with gratitude. Having mercy for your soft, animal body capable of feeling so much sadness; moving out of freeze and chaos. As I moved through my grief, I started to notice myself soften; I noticed the first true bursts of joy I'd felt in a long time. When we invite ourselves to soften, we are able to notice the joy in simple presence and patiently allow that sensation to build over time. My drama storm started to have clear sunny days. I finally started to understand why people cry when they experience joy.

There is faint pleasure in enjoying solitude once you realize you have finally successfully befriended yourself. Gratitude for each tiny win or joyful bite of life. Being alone feels less often like loneliness and more often like peace. There are inside jokes with yourself and God. You enjoy a warm, buttery croissant and allow all the flakes to fall in your lap. Softness and solitude are a recipe for befriending your inner child, who merely desires for you to play with her and pay attention to her. It doesn't always need to be fancy.

Softness is central to one of my favorite practices, which has helped me stretch. That is, making silly, innocent, ugly art — giving my poems, paintings, or anything permission to be bad. The fun thing about this is that freedom is all you really need to build the muscle, yet sometimes when you look back, you can feel that what your play yielded was truth and raw expression. Therein lies its beauty, and you sigh at ever having judged it. Even overbaked cookies are still wholesome and delicious. Finding awe in simplicity is no small feat; it is the strongest source of resilience.

Soft

The tree by my window is blooming; the sun is shining in the city
I am self-aware enough to know my grip on reality has been looser
I grasp for my usual lifelines, embracing a shift
Ran the laundry and forgot the soap
Read one page of my book; forty-five minutes passed
Grass, like eyelashes, pebbles, freckles
My toe is bruised and painful, but I know I am well
As well as I've ever been and ripe for change
Not the kind that knocks you over and rips your heart
Change that wraps you in a warm breeze
It holds your hand as you surrender

Clearing Away

I have to create meaning or I'll wash away with the high tide
I must push past my fears, or I'll never forgive myself

Cast my needs to the angels
Goddess, anchor me to steady
Bracing the swells that threaten to pull me under
This voyage has a purpose
It has to mean release

Lightning strikes, and I'm waiting for the boom
Counting the seconds as miles mark the thunder

Between one storm and the next, I am simply in the eye
Resting between my pupils where I can't yet see
I have to tell myself to exhale into the electricity

My desires may feel like heartache, but I love to dance in the rain
Feel it clearing away

Warmth

I decided
to be the type of person who showed up
The trees are still emerging from winter
Green moss creeps up their sides
And peaked buds whisper promises
I started loving rain when it left me feeling warm
And cleared the streets of sorrow
Warm wind fills my lungs with the jasmine I choose to dream of
Magnolias blooming on my block, in your garden, at the cemetery
Make it ice cream — make it mean something
Days of sun are coming sure as tomorrow
Sweat beads down your chest to your navel
Center of all creation, balance
Sunburns warm your heart in darkness
That is love; that is reason to grin
Love letters for all things saccharine
The moon is always changing shape
Nothing is ever really lost
The crocuses that brought you hope are past their time
Daffodils are here now and won't last
We believe in the resurrection, as there is evidence all around us
That all endings are beginnings
That all seasons beget love
Black and white
All the colors at rest in the in-between
Bring vibrancy to our days
Bring that familiar warmth

Morning Dew

River of emotions pulls me back into the past

A Time Machine

I gasp for air in the rip-tide

Wait to be deposited back upon the shore

The present, where you're gone, but overwhelmingly

I'm here

Undulating and turned on in ways I thought I'd forgotten —

Further into primal self-expression

Transcending ways I've ever allowed myself to move in the waves

Those tiny white bulbous flowers where fairies live, and I rest

Drinking morning dew, I return to myself

Held each day by deep commitment to her

On the shores of the present

Caressed by the petals nearing full bloom

The Waiting

The darkness of winter begins to lift
The sun shines, warming my skin
Still, the breeze brings goosebumps to full attention
I want to scoop up the spirits of each face I see

Strangers burdened by so many layers of failure
None of which is their own, still they'll bear the cross
So I pray and pray that we collectively learn
Presence and individualism will not save the world

You cannot save the world without saving everyone in it
Especially those you don't have the privilege of knowing
Despite all the privilege you stand upon
Saving you from their circumstance

Forty days until spring, and a mother heals from her initiation
Inward and tending to an innocent being with care
Let me hold your heart through the waiting
There is no promise of resurrection in the snow

The birds chirping and buds on the trees
Fill me with such bone deep optimism
On the other side
Of whatever we are carrying now

Blue Jay

I look to the sky for answers, and I hear the singing birds
If I see a blue jay following me, I know it will all be okay

We seek signs that we are heading in the right direction
But there are cinnamon rolls and questionable punctuation
I wanted to see above the treetops, but I slid under the protection of
the canopy for safety
I plan to evaluate from here just how high I can climb

Hope brings me to my knees as I feel my desires inching towards me
Scooping up the tadpoles and fearing something is wrong,
I'm praying to the swirling tide pools that never rest for stillness
A stream, not a glassy lake, trickles towards the pond

The gravity we feel and the topography we think we see
I know of several contradictions, yet with hope
I'm convinced anything could be

Strawberry Ice Cream

I woke up at 3pm

I left my bed for strawberry ice cream

A balmy wind blew as a saxophone band played in the park

I wasn't sure if it was music I heard or my own brain fog soundtrack

I watched them, and I licked quickly so my treat wouldn't melt down my cone and hand

I thought to reach for my phone, but some peaceful pockets of life are too sweet to tamper with

I think of how my heart is both a grown woman and a teenage girl all at once

Red Lipstick

I'm wearing red lipstick to honor my ancestors
They're protecting me from a faucet of sorrow

I've lost a few friends once they met my family
Not because of their many flaws
But because of our love despite them all

It's deeply unfamiliar to many, I've found, and that knowing fills me
        with deep gratitude
Our casual togetherness and joy in closeness

It's one thing to focus on healing generational wounds and another
        to rest in the gifts
The values that have transcended lifetime and circumstance

Her abiding hope was that we love and care for one another
To keep the hearth of the fire lit to gather around —
to not let it go cold in her absence

For that to be the provenance of a woman who carried so much
        speaks volumes
Literally through our bones and my fingertips
The matriarchs who honored tradition and embodied grace

Love, like wealth, like class, is not something that can be bought
It is taught
In our grandmothers' doilies, quaffed hair, and kisses

It is inscribed on our hearts in bright red lipstick

Change the World

I know that we can change the world
I've changed the world I live in
It's why I now weep at sunsets and silly bits

The world where my belonging in it was a distant fantasy
Cold and gray
Assuming the worst in a constant barrage of negative projections
Don't speak to me; I am a cactus
      and I've been stabbed ten thousand times
I'm in so much pain I'll hurt you too and I'm terrified

One more failed friend could turn and I'd meet my end
There have been several sad wells I thought I'd never climb out of
I thought maybe this damp world wasn't worth it
My tears could fill the space and float me to safety

I walk down the streets and instead of garbage I notice disco balls
and a child giggling
I sung with strangers and the charge was transmuted into hope
I strutted into the party and smiled wide with an open heart
I introduced myself to everyone and called them by their names

Sounds so simple, doesn't it? To have an open heart
Able to see myself, I notice my own shock in their mirrored embrace
I live in a different world, I changed my world

By changing our world, we change the world around us
Healing our capacity to love, starting with ourselves
      blankets the whole world in it
Those of us, the chronically misunderstood, know how incredible it
is to simply love

Shared Meals

I don't take it for granted

The nights spent in laughter with others

The giggles and jokes that become memories, like a secret love letter

Spaces and moments where you are unrestrained

Authenticity comes easily as spreading softened butter
Across fresh, warm toast

Inhibitions go to the wayside
And there is no fear of judgment or ridicule
Only silliness, only play

Moments to sink your teeth into and dive into simple pleasures

No performance, unless one feels right, of course

To be savored like fine wine

I know what it is to starve

Hardcore Softness

I think I'm going to kill her
The part of me still begging for your approval
Little girl playing dress up in technicolor glasses

Show me something real
Have you ever been so lost there seems to be nowhere to go?

A million tiny daggers
Muscle spasms and shortened breath
Calm down; you're doing your best
Screaming on the inside and nausea out my nose

I keep trying to close the door behind us
Your little phrases slip through my lips
And I tumble back into the sheets

A lover holds my hand as I wept in a way you never would
Bracing myself against the penetration of my spirit
Admitting it felt weak, but today it feels like strength
Your words, like knives, that flayed my nerve endings

Grieving now a version of myself
Molded like marzipan
One flavor, any shape you please
Discipline. Routine. Don't compromise now.
Hardcore softness.

You can only swallow your pride so many times before you swallow
your self

Whole

RAGE

When I started writing and doing therapeutic parts work, separating and labeling my emotions, I didn't know much about the mythological and literary trope of dragons. I merely discovered my dragon in trying to understand and develop a relationship with my anger. My rage lights me up; it sets me on fire; it tells me who I am. It reminds me of what I stand for, how I expect to be treated, and what really matters to me. It is my power, and I had to train it so as to not burn down entire communities or keep me locked in a tower. I learned to ride on her back and kiss her gently on the mouth. Most of the time these days when she's excited, I'm positively tickled because I'm turned on. Sometimes we simply need to blow off steam and rage cry at all the injustices and unfairness in the world. We burn down all the wildflowers in our wake, knowing we all need it and everything will grow again.

We need to say what we feel and what we think, and in that sense, rage is a reminder that we are still alive. The spark of fight is not dead within us. We are mother lions roaring and ripping the head off of anyone who dares to threaten our young, rightfully so. We call it justice; women are belittled for being angry, yet it is the most natural, innate reaction when we need our ferocity to be seen and respected.

I've experienced a lot of anger at feeling betrayed, misunderstood, and wronged by others. The most devastating anger, however, is the anger that I directed at myself — mostly out of shame for actions or lack of actions, for being stuck, or for making a mistake. There is a dance of rage and forgiveness. The agitation that can only be cooled with appropriate release and great grace. Pain is a tremendous portal, and what is rage but an expression of extreme pain?

Throughout much of my life, my anger was uncontrollable. It ruined so many relationships and resulted in actions that made me deeply ashamed, which in turn kicked up more anger. As a child I was punished for having big feelings of any variety, so I learned to push them down, hide them. Well, they would eventually all come out with a roar. An outburst that would inevitably end in more punishment. A cycle that would continue until I learned as an adult how to regulate my emotions, which turns out is largely just giving yourself permission to experience them.

When I was in college, I drank a lot, in an attempt to fit in. I was a really cool and funny drunk, until I wasn't. Sometimes the poison would release my untamed dragon, like all the rage I'd pushed down and buried had broken out of its cage with a vengeance.

There are somatic releases I do now that have helped heal the version of myself who didn't know better. In many ways, simple containment with permission to feel has saved my life. My dragon didn't know where to put her anger, and when it arose, it spread like a wildfire she couldn't put out. She didn't know how to repair and rebuild. I didn't know how to approach conflict from a calm, empowered, and loving place. I had to learn how to allow conflict to deepen intimacy rather than destroy it. I didn't know the big, big, big feelings were just energy. Rage is sacred. Rage is necessary. You are often right to be angry.

Walk the tightrope between letting your dragon not be tamed (you cannot cage it) and creating appropriate space for her to breathe fire. Rage can burn all the bridges in your life, or it can show you which ones to take.

Live Laugh Love

Judging your live laugh love as I clench my jaw
It's tacky, and I don't believe you
Without the depth of repeated initiation
Tumbling in the dryer
You can't know how right you are

To know the feminine longing to be dressed by little birds
        as you sing in the morning
To feel the breeze and the warm sun on your vulva
        greeting this world anew
To nurture with compassion, with dangerous ease

Relish in the sensual beauty this life offers
From delighting in a rose to engulfing a man
All pleasures risk impermanence
A small papercut
An invasive surgery

Love comes naturally and lasts forever
Unconditional
Prayerful gaze, authentic giggles
Divinely, strictly, determined, and earned
Glitter glue on mundane moments

Nourishment of a home-cooked meal
The gentle, slow, soothing caress of a partner

The cages we build to hold the birds
        only to grow annoyed by their song

Listening to the sirens wail, echoing in my solitude
A pristine tower for one

Away from,
Alone with,
Pain

A dull headache and aching teeth
Stuck in a vice grip
Quiet mornings with a sword in my chest

The birds sing
Tears drain layers of shame
A gnawing reminder of my gorgeously fragile heart

Cracked like an egg
Scrambled with cheese
Made with love

I soak in a golden bathtub
Brushing oils through my hair
Remembering I am perfection
Adorning myself with praise
Repeatedly, routinely, cultivating joy
Louder every day

The sun reaches my face
I remember I too am fire
What a hilarious circus

Live
Laugh
Love

The Choice

I made a promise to myself

When he still had his grip around my throat —

When his cunning smile could still spread my legs —

When he still told me where to be and when —

When I still used the fuses of my dimmed power to send all my prayers to God for him and his benefit alone —

Never my own

When I sat staring at an unrecognizable sweet-little-self in the mirror and finally saw my bigness in the brokenness

When I felt my heart being birthed out of my throat with splitting pain

The winding path was only twofold in the end

You'll either

Be with him forever; savor this love despite the misery

Or

Be more yourself than you can ever imagine and live this life free

Marry him for the phantom frozen picture frame life now

Or

Fuck it all up

Because fuck you,

You know there is more for you than this

Life stretches far beyond the canvas of that pretty picture

Go prove it to yourself

What Shook My Reality

I'd like to say it was sudden and cute
Evocative, a magical succinct tale
Clean fondant; no seams with painted woodland creatures

It was an ugly slug being dragged
Splayed naked on a stone to sacrifice
Left to rot in a ditch it took years to climb out of

So blessed, truly, to be sheltered
A bubble of impenetrable glass for the soul
Sweet brainwashing to fit a brutal reality
Conveyer belt dreams and cliques in matching costume

I confess, it seems I am always in this process of becoming
Exploring more deeply my pleasures and passions
Holding all that I am and inspecting it with care
There is profound prophecy in solitude
The way is clear when you're no one's prey

A jaguar saunters in its corner of the forest
No one dare underestimate its supple brutality

Still no animal belongs in a cage
Even if they've long forgotten about the Amazon
Never forget your animal body
You're an overdeveloped pretentious ape

I Wouldn't Wait

If I could do it again, I wouldn't wait
For the paperwork to be drawn up
The check to clear with the legal team
For them to double check my grammar
For anything that makes me feel like self-flagellation

I wouldn't wait for some abstract future where I feel more alive
I'd sink my teeth into whatever felt good and made me laugh
I would put all of my focus on what I want to grow
Let it unravel and reveal its potential
This precious life is for my pleasure

Eroticize a grilled cheese sandwich
Sip mint tea on the back porch in the rain
Make different kinds of love in every room of the house
Lose count of all the times we came

Write poems and rip them up in a fit
Tape them back together and post them on the internet
Decide everyday conversations are sacred
Because they are, if you anoint them as such

This party is a comedy skit
A contemporary dance performance
You've already bought tickets, and I'm making a fortune
I'm paid to exist; my eros is abundance

You don't need anyone or anything to start
Loving

Kingdom

Simmering
My hairs stand up on my skin
Rosemary oil and a tingling scalp
Somehow, I've become a tiger

A transition and a fight
Changing colors and cortisol spikes
I need so much time to do nothing
And I'm so tired of it

Spiders up my sternum, weaving a web
Where my soul sits now
The rightful heir to the kingdom
On its journey home
Inevitable, but unbeknownst to her

Second nature
Spinning the wool to make the string
Adorned with garments
Beads stitched in
Painstakingly

Kicking and screaming
Through the quicksand
To the precipice of destiny

A jaguar prowls
Queen of the night
One paw over the other
The treetops her throne

I Plan to Forgive Her

I cried myself awake
A simple dream of isolation
A fear of getting too close, only for it all to be taken away

Tremors as I approached the Tarot cards
They called me over to comfort me
The others claimed it wasn't my place
I did not hold that magic in their eyes

I'd misspoken or mis-stepped
I was out, and there was no door back in
I wasn't part of it
I learned it was safer that way
Much better to be on the fray

What do we have here?
You'll never be understood
Nobody wants to see you
Be seen with you
You really are that hard to love

I follow the feeling
Like a river carving canyons
I let it flow through me
Until I shook myself awake

Crying in my peaceful little room
Where my deepest wounds crawl in through my ears as I sleep
And I wake again to love myself a little bit harder

Going to bed angry
In a lover's quarrel with myself

In the morning, I plan to forgive her

What Makes You Scream?

Failed driver's test
Can't finish the exam in time, but I know all the answers

He fucked another girl
Everyone is hanging out without me

What makes you scream?
Do you scream like you fucking mean it?
I know my scream shakes the whole world
Booms and aftershocks and devastation

I erupt like a volcano
Unexpected from the small ocean reef
Lava flowing out from the core
As she becomes as big as her energy feels

When I scream, I trigger everyone who's ever known me
A natural disaster, and you can't look away
From the sheer power of nature before you
Magnificent and rare

I laugh softly, loving this woman I used to hate
Smirking
I'm so hot
Like a volcano

Warm and Fuzzies

In my body is a chaos storm
I wanted you to hold me together so I could rest
My arms luckily had learned to do it myself by then
Pushed away again, again, again

I spend all day crying
Paint my nails holographic chrome
Old-fashioned elegance is costume jewelry
I dress myself in polka dots and sunbeams

Due to personal reasons
I will no longer be making jokes about being delusional

Fall air brings freshness
These fantasies must be left to the summer

Fireflies in glass jars seeking pleasure
Play that must be set free

Hand me a needle
I release the pressure without a rupture
See my heart beating as it leaks into the vial

It's all love, but if it's not Love
Reciprocity and sweetness
I never learned how to knit
I'll need to before the next hurricane

Tomorrow is for warm and fuzzies
I can't face the tide without sufficient yarn

Fire Breathing Dragon

The last thing I want to do is recoil
Showing up to be judged — to be slain like some hideous beast
      who dares bare its teeth
A fire breathing dragon in chains of illusion
Wings clipped by the ferocity of storytelling
Caged and tamed by shame
I am not an iguana or a bird
What am I?
How dare I exist in a reality other than the one that pacifies you?
I growl at the lies and propaganda designed to hold me in
The opposite of dysregulation is not subordinance or silence
The opposite of belonging is not shrinking to fit your mold
Eventually the mystic must accept the sweeping sensation
Let the air catch beneath the scales up her back
Stretch out into the space that calls her
The land where logic and fantasy meet
Don't be surprised if you see a dragon soar overhead

Chaos Confetti

The way it goes

You lay all your cards on the table

You turn over the one you've been waiting for

A giggle of glee escapes your lips

Your opponents know something is about to erupt

You shock them all by ripping the card into a thousand tiny pieces

Toss the remains and destroy anything the ashes touch

Chaos confetti rains down, and the board is clear

The thrill of creating destruction

One-time use that changes everything for you

This is how you shoot your shot

Starting over

Space Queen

Crown of the cosmos
Elements vibrating in my orbit
I stand at the center of my own universe
I'm lightyears away from my moon phase
Under pressure, I did not remain stone
I exploded into flames
Attracting matter and praying for life
Stars shine brightest in the dark

Holy Fire

Holy fire in you
There is a gloom that can be healed with it
On Easter, we are asked to go and tell
Share that every child of God is loved and worthy

There is no correct way to live; it's all about choices
Balance of action, choosing, and also surrender

Like love, we never regret doing most things
Even if love ends in pain, lessons, and a deep need for being
Thank God it happened

The Loudest Screams

Retreating to a wooden playhouse
I can see them, but no harm can reach me
There is something about that feeling
I knew I'd carry it my whole life

Hit me with a tambourine
Make beauty from the abuse of being alive
The echo of my melancholia makes a melody
My hips shake as I hold myself in quivering embrace

Dating is not an option with a vulnerable heart
Careful in your pursuit; I'll try to give it all to you
I've hidden hurt behind anger
Disguised my love as lust

My reflection: a girl I've been
Polka-dot tube top performance
Seeking attention, affection, acceptance
I'm here giving it to you

A fairy in blue tulle spins around in solitude —
Splashes in the puddle of tears she didn't cry
The loudest screams are the ones laced with angst
They reach a soundless decibel

Emotional Sobriety

If I think too long, I can still taste it
Smell its musk and the warm sensation that rushed through my veins
      when I swallowed
The pill that lit me on fire and made me fall to my knees
I lay in a stupor going through the motions
Excuses as priorities and putting off living
High each waking hour, lost following the compulsion to catch a hit
The highs, the highs, oh the lows
As I hug the toilet, trying to remember
Visuals spinning I'm convinced are real
I feel it still if I sit long enough for the bitterness
I swallow my own spit and know sobriety suits me well
It clears with a cough — a shout — and it melts under my tongue
Into my core, and the tingle of my own supply returns
Honey, caramel, mercury, lead
Grandmother holds me in a prayer and cleanses me with tears
Close and forgotten pride, in slowly, finally, letting this go

PROTECTORS

There is a part of me that is a small chipmunk, frozen, shaking, and afraid to take up space. Another that is a jaguar, balanced, agile, lethal. My regal, mature, erotic and commanding presence that gently establishes the rules with which she will be met. She guards my sense of safety and protects me.

Our protectors establish and hold our boundaries as sacred. Quivering into submission and making myself as small as possible was a learned defense mechanism. One which my protector honors without shame. Knowing that part needs kindness to feel safe to transform and evolve.

If I ever second-guessed my decision to end my last relationship, the reminder is in memories of people questioning how quiet I was around him. How I came to embody that small chipmunk skittering through the forest. It is also in the lapses of memory from that period of my life. Though it was long before I met him that I learned how painful it felt to be misunderstood, to not be seen. I'd been told I was way too much and hard to be friends with. If you're told that often enough, you will start to believe it, at least a little. This inhibition, however, even predates those times. This assignment is womb-deep — literally — from when I was squished in my mother's womb, where my twin sister took up most of the space. I say this only to explain why my healing absolutely needed to be somatic. I needed to listen to my body, to complete the stress responses I'd packed carefully inside, to learn where I was not free, what I needed to express, to feel my power.

It is in feeling our own bodily sensations and posture that we learn, are shown, where our boundaries have been crossed and need to be established. There are to be no silent expectations or transgressions unaddressed. In establishing boundaries around the small moments, the first feelings of disrespect, you can learn a lot about how people will treat you. Particularly in dating, you can weed out those who get defensive and try to become the victim, or people who try to find creative ways around your boundaries. Both reactions allude to manipulation and control, for which I have a zero-tolerance policy.

Trusting yourself enough to use your voice and make decisions starts with being willing and able to stand up for yourself. Learning to do so from a place of respect. Women are taught to people please and be accommodating — I was actually very bad at this until I was taught my lack of compliance was a flaw. I have reclaimed it as a gift, the wildness of my being, knowing my own truth. In this truth I am elegant and sultry, a beautiful alluring threat to anyone who tries to fuck with me. It is such a soft and pleasurable power, knowing your own worth.

When we allow people to treat us as less than the magnificent creatures we are, we do ourselves a great injustice. When people treat you like you are not a fully autonomous person with a life that is as valuable and rich as theirs, they dehumanize you. Anyone who continues to make me feel unsafe, who cannot see how hard I am working to protect myself, is not welcome to keep meeting with the soft and gentle parts of my soul. They will be removed by the jaguar.

Katana

I didn't just draw a katana
I etched it deep into metal with a knife
I printed it in a black ink relief
Applied extreme pressure over and over

I didn't know when
I gave it to him as a gift
It would courageously sever the bond
A final battle of honor

Unlace the chains of this corset
That keeps my breath shallow
As much a warrior as your princess
Weapons to hang on your wall

I armor up with a katana
Strapped down my sternum
Where I need it most

Structural integrity for my ribcage
So my heart stops falling out

May men cut their hands on sharp blades
Who try to hurt me

He gave the print back to me in the end
A trophy of protection

Tending the Garden

The crick in my back arises to distract me
Aches, I'm alive, I'm alive and need tending
Like the fruit in your garden
Needs to be harvested when ripe
Or they'll rot and the white filaments of death will spread
Through your raspberries
Praying to be eaten by wild animal bellies
Bear our fruit and let the seeds complete their aching for bees
To turn hard work into the despair of honey farmers
All the sweetness seemingly for nothing
Making enough, always enough, and somehow more
Sow the garden you have planted and pull the weeds
A part of me yelps, "they belong"
Unintended beauty, green, still life
Delicate petal saplings I pull and release
Wheat is begging to bear its potential
Grinding in the moving mill to churn to flour
Once I let it wait for the right time to die

Confessions

My throat is constricted
You can never hurt me if I never meet you

I saw a picture of him, and it no longer matches my memory
It seems I no longer know who I've created to ache about
All longing has the terrifying reality of being for the future

Years ago, words started pouring out of me
A faucet I'd turned on
I tapped it out and filled my lungs from there
I don't know what I'm running from anymore
or what I'm writing about

Can I confess to sex dreams about Jesus?
That I feel anger towards anyone freer than I'll allow for me?
Candlelit courage and copper balls
I'm in the city, and that must suffice for a bonfire
The ones I imagine myself playing the guitar around
Singing the songs I'd sung with you

Love Against All Odds

I haven't been creating but contracting
Blooming, I found myself shriveled in a thicket of thorns
Here again, familiar frost
It's August, but the wall I've built shades eternal winter
Sickening sweetness, watermelon sprinklers
Gardenias for my grandmother and roses whisper prayers
The bite of wind against my wings speaks remembrance
The plants remain; this bush does not cease to be a rose
The devotion doesn't die; love longs for us in all seasons
Gather warmth from the roots that hold us all

Be held by Mother Earth, who blessed you with monthly ritual
I need to express, otherwise the teen angst will build up
Write sad songs, if you must, but let it out of you
On paper or through movement
Draw a bath, play, reclaim your innocence

I always contract the most before I expand
Restriction darling
You asked to be set free
You know what you need to do next
Take up space; don't stay small
Reveal the truth of all that you are

Love against all odds, embarrassing
You deserve to allow yourself to use your voice
Express yourself fully without being shut down
Open your heart, tight jaw, clenched pelvis
I collapse into the void so I can blossom anew
What poison am I drinking?
Where am a lying to myself, calling it medicine?

Lollipop

My protectors need to be carefully caressed
They need my gentle encouragement to soften

The lightest, unexpecting touch
The width of my tongue
To trust me to hold my boundaries while opening

To the creative, loving force that bubbles over
The joy that is allowing myself to not be filtered

My thick, impenetrable coating of sugar
Pushing away my purpose when it feels too big

Hard, frozen sugar that needs to melt
Or be licked gently, patiently, away

The tingle like smelling pepper in my sinuses before I cry
In my home, I am safe to feel slowly
Small pieces of candy I can resource with
Memories of freedom as touchstones

Took It Too Far

I went too far
I climbed to the top
I fell off the edge
From where your love left me
To where I was waiting
I must have missed something
In gathering all my missing pieces
Exalted by their safe return, I dropped it
From craving validation from you to avoiding the risk of it all
I thought it wise to allow my bearded dragon to guard my heart
She is blue, with silver hair and iridescent scales
And she'll breathe fire down on anyone who dares get close to me
I love her, and I know intimacy
And I know I've never known intimacy
The kind I know to be real, from fable to fantasy
The confidence is written across my chest
Behind it — a girl weeping poetry
I went too far
Took it too far
Right past the point of stability
My fears in control
Forgot the kingdom of security
And I fell
Further
I fell
Even further away from my love

The Highest Shelf

I took my love and put it on the highest shelf
Where I'd have to grab my dining stool and scoot it to stand on
I knew I wouldn't be needing it for a while
I took a hot bath to steep in
Took extra care to wash each inch of flesh
Wiggled my fingers between each toe
Rubbing gently to soften the calluses that built these hardened edges
Walking the streets in the rain
That often brings comfort, but today was supposed to be May
And yesterday
The chill pierced me
And the muse called me into the waters
Her siren song so sweet
Dragged down into the depths
Maybe the horseshoe effect applies to my heart
If I reach, I'll touch it
I'll find my love lies just beneath the surface

It Shines for You Too

I was spitting fire yesterday
You left, and I felt the evaporation
As my warmth returned to the surface

I'm almost guilty for holding my ground
Bracing myself against your heavy wind

Compassion comes to mind as I hear your soft wilting
Drowning in water but refusing sunshine

Stop talking; start feeling
It shines for you too — I promise

Ice cubes melting into a puddle beside me
I finally dried off, cozy and warm

I'll be with you, but I won't go there with you
I hope you understand this is love too

Singing Softly

Singing softly
To be heard above a whisper
Tell me lies
Tell me secrets
Any truth I can believe in
Sometimes forward seems like backward
Looks the same, but it's all different
Change of seasons for being
Singing softly for attic walls and moth balls
With freedom from weighted reputation
The world spins faster
My momentum builds too
The projectile split from orbit, making one of its own
Singing softly for fur ears and fairies
For the friends suffering uncertainty
   the cruel companion of real freedom
   soothed only by soft lullabies
Followed by expression from appreciation of what brought you here
Refusing self-abandonment for the mere tolerance that left you mute
To sing softly to the echoing walls of an 18th-century stable
Freedom comes in many flavors, and you're allowed to try them all
To suck the bones on the hard-earned version of success that fills
you up

Decisions

The whirlwind of making a decision
Feeling two futures making themselves available

Arms and legs wide open to embrace me
The longer you wait, the less cute your eventual surrender

Not a passionate sweep but a relinquished bow
I sit at my desk, in this spot, with excitement and in mourning

So ready, but so safe here in this moment
A woodpecker bangs against my ribcage

I can't wait to sip coffee with wet toes in the grass
Watching the birds who sang us awake

Hair

He wanted me to cut my hair
told me he'd hold me closer
Better if I had a pixie cut —
to match my petite frame
for his pleasure —
match his fantasies
a new style
a new start

I remember when I dyed my hair blonde —
in fear and panic as I felt my self
shrinking
Bleached my soul in the void in search of safety
my biggest critic did not approve
I grasped for something to hold onto —
to hide behind
I cut it short again, I dyed it red
The red wash faded, and I looked burnt
Everyone could see my pain —
exposed and damaged

My hair is graying, and I let it grow long
I don't pull them out

Years passed and the damage grew out
It now hangs down to my waist
covers my breasts
I wrap myself in it
I am safe
More importantly
I look like me

To Love Yourself Well

There is a task that is not rewarded in our society
It is blanketed in placating cliches of bubble baths
And cucumbers on your eyes
To love yourself well is a deeply intimate affair

A vulnerability and a safety that can only exist between yourself and
you

We applaud those who find a partner because they have
accomplished the externalized accreditation

What I want to know is how much time you have spent with your
fingers inside yourself,
feeling the pleasure and pain of your moist gooey center

I want to know if you've held yourself while you cried, until you
thought you might vomit

I want to know if you look in the mirror and blow yourself a kiss

Partnership is beautiful, but you must first love yourself all the way
Otherwise, you will hit a limit
Of how deeply you can love and be loved by another

No one can praise you enough for you to believe it
Praise be to God

Tell yourself you deserve everything you've ever wanted
Fight for it fiercely and risk being good

Then go remind a friend

Pied Piper

Don't fight your nature singing to you softly
The pied piper leading you into the jungle of fate
Each person you meet
A reminder that I'm waiting for you
I'm speaking wisdom into the nerves of your teeth
Sending shivers through your veins, saying, "Wake up"
The hearts of the world beat better with you in it
The peace, the sex, the beauty this life offers
You're famished for meaning, and I can satiate you
There is no price, no prize to be won for fighting it now
Hiding in a bunker is not safety without threat
The war is over; I know it raged on for years
The war is over; lay down your fears
Refuse to die now
Act now; realize that no external source will knight you
Pedestal you and praise you for figuring it out
You're insane. Good.
Real sanity will never seem to make sense in this world

Sepia-Toned

Stillness and solitude allow space to hear
      There is a false safety in silence
I can romanticize a sepia-toned photograph
      I would be lying if I didn't express how much I wish
      it were in full color
To see the world in full saturation or pastel shine

With deep study of myself, I have been made aware of each knot
that holds me bound
The way my ego protects me through judgment
The way that judgment makes me hold back my love
Isn't that the funniest thing?
      Hiding one's heart when it yearns to hold
      and be held

To be seen in its fullness and the truth of its experience
The burden of beliefs, like stones upon my altar
Are now crystallized to keep me stuck in place
Waiting on my prayers to liquify and turn back to molten

I tell myself they are those of others, gifts kept with guilt
      but they are mine
I alone am able to turn them into gold
      to purify my path to liberation
There comes a point where rest becomes counterproductive
When action is the only way free

Grit

Good grit
I'm feeling a little wild
So I may make out in the corner
With the questions that weigh on my heart
Learn to flirt with the guards who hold her
The remaining parts of me, hidden so well

Sweet Raspberry Jam

A primordial scream oozes from my core — ugly and messy and raw
A jam jar shatters on the floor, and the sweetness looks like blood
The last of the bottle, a tube, and I'm squeezing out this feeling
Energetically heaving from the center of my being
My pores are sweating as I'm wrung out with unspeakable sorrow
My pain, your grief, our suffering, collective
I lick the sticky berries up off the floor
A practice of devotion and prayer
Each of my mistakes delicious
Beautiful reminders of how close joy is
A choice and an allowance
A softening deeper into emotion so it may
Finally flow out and feel complete
Cleaned up clarity, empty
Empty so you may fill
Space for joy
Capacity
Ease

EXPANSION

Contracting and expanding, forever and ever.

I am very petite, and my personality always felt so much bigger than my external expression. I continually felt I was being asked to take up even less and less space, share my space, or shrink when I already felt squished by societal and familial expectations of who I am.

So much of my ability to take up space and express myself as an adult has been in healing my inner child — allowing her desires to exist, letting her make a mess, be a beginner, and explore with full permission. I have become a huge proponent of being mediocre at things. This world loves telling people they can only act in the pursuit of excellence or money, but that is no fun at all. Taking on a new hobby or learning for the sake of it, helps us to expand and to tap into childlike wonder and curiosity that enriches us.

I was raised in a family that regularly had casual sing-a-longs and dance parties. Enjoying each other's company in lighthearted fun. I remember a handful of times when I sat quietly watching. The times I noticed that I could not allow myself to join in, even though I wanted to. I could not participate and that needed to change. As I healed, little by little I could feel free again, maybe more so than I ever had. I now revel in those moments with a deeper gratitude.

People say they can't do karaoke because they "can't sing." That is not the point, and everyone can sing as long as they can create sound. It's inhibitions and contraction and fear — the kind of fear that in some situations genuinely keeps us safe, but other times holds us back from raw pleasures of existing. Pleasure that is always right there for you to reach out and grab, if you so choose. I will never go back to living in a silent film.

Expansion is the confrontation of fear in the pursuit of joy.

The key to reparenting yourself is healing your relationship between you, yourself, and your faith. Like a child who needs a secure parent to thrive, you need to be able to be your own primary attachment figure — and in doubt, be able to orient to a higher power. Be your own safe space to return to each time you engage with risk. Allow the divine to be the arms always with you — the ones you rest in. This relationship keeps the promise with yourself and God of unconditional love and acceptance through your imperfect journey.

From here you can take the small steps, allowing yourself to step outside of your comfort zone in alignment with your desires. Pushing the edges of your window of tolerance is uncomfortable, and it's worth it.

Plan for it, sign up for the class, book the trip, set an intention to do the thing that feels just a little scary. I don't mean skydiving if that's not true to you. I mean doing that thing you've been putting off, waiting for a different version of you to reach for. We must not fear joy — the emotions that come up as you live must be felt. I'll cry in my art class and navigate the anxiety of flying. Expansion is not comfortable, no growth is; it requires change. Changing yourself by being yourself. Expansion is opening more to who you are, to your life, to being alive.

Big

I have a thin membrane between me and the bigness I crave
Big love
Big joy
Big purpose
Big abundance
Big community

And so I have to show up
I have to dance through it
Sing vows of praise to my god
Small acts, each a step to speed up the healing
Make myself able to carry all the feeling

Create capacity
Get BIG

Alto

The song hit a pitch I couldn't sing
My voice cracked trying to reach the notes like a whisper

Deep alto reverberates through my soul
And needs to be released with a dance

They wanted me to write a blog that felt like a grocery list
I winced as they scraped off even the mildest seasonings I'd added

He wanted a woman he could wear like an accessory
Not even bedazzled with bold beading to reflect the light

I didn't fit that mold, and trust me I tried
Like a Great Dane on a chihuahua's bed

I realized in time how laughable an attempt it was
To be anything but myself
And all of the bigness I'd timidly tucked behind my ear

I was 10 years old when I took the stage
Singing at the foot of my parents' bed
        when they encouraged me to do the audition

I'll never forget the way they looked at each other
        with knowing smiles
I got the part; of course I did
I was so big before I learned to be small

You Are My Everything

That old wooden ball game on tracks —
We're ascending the spiral until a part of me falls —
Falls back in love for a moment and cries out to hold you close

I wish things were different
That we were together and in love
That my nervous system could have healed
        from the persistent rattling
That I could have trusted you to care for my heart
        but I couldn't

I never wanted this for us
I wanted to heal together; I really did
After everything, I don't love you any less
I only love myself more

Pillows nuzzled against New York City windows, safe and snug
Falling to your death

I started preschool before I could talk
It would take me another 27 years to learn the power of my voice
The only sound that can heal me
Its poignancy creates my new reality

"You are my everything," she whispers to herself
Eyes squinting at the horizon
"I'm ready for something to begin"

I have been my most brutal tormentor
Healing meant removing anyone who added to that burden
I'd rather be alone than not be held like a glass vase
        with the reverence of a cherished gift

You can't change the narrative in your mind
If those closest to you continually reinforce it
I hand you back your tray of criticism and disappointment
I'm sorry you're hurting too

I'm praying to you, and well with tears
I'm seeking, and I'll never stop seeking
I feel your love wrapped around me; it's tethering me to this Earth
Safe here to relish in the searching

Bathe in my waters and fill your cup
Fill yourself up over and over

What Did This Teach Me?

My blood sugar's spiking
I feel it climbing
From my toes to my nose
My head is heavy and aching
My mouth, still salivating
A pitted ache in my gut
Full of what my mouth wanted
What is being immediately rejected
Whoopie pie
Not just any kind —
banana bread, squishy cookie bookends
Fluffy sugar filling I licked, then devoured
I cut it in half
but ate them both
What did this teach me?

Uncomfortable

Uncomfortable —
      like a snake emerging from its old, ashen skin

Using one of those special knives for delicately slicing cheese
      on my raw flesh

There are layers to get down to that part of me,
      stuck in the cave screaming for relief

Endure the digging

I Judged Her

God, I pray to go off the rails
Again and again
To wake up
to the deeper truth

She lost possession of her faculties
Lost access to all that was rightfully hers
Separating from the image you're sold as correct
Is the deepest sanity

Validation and belonging are addictive
She wore her heart on her sleeve
If love is a battlefield, what is pride?
What is grief and faith?

Perhaps a warm bath
or a field of flowers to lay in
No bugs

Before I learned how to think for myself
Saw the woman she had to be to survive
Felt that same ache of desperation in my bone marrow

Did I realize how brave she was?
Doing her best?
I judged her
Just like everybody else

The Beast

Let them see the beast and chuckle at its size
She will eat them, swallow them whole, either way

There is no domestication for what you were born to be
No convincing you there is any other worthwhile pursuit
No cage nor zoo can hold the vastness of your heart

Make her cry; you'll need an ark
Make her scream; the world trembles to its core
Tell her you love her and watch as flowers bloom around you
Engage her mind; feel lightning strike between you
Touch her skin and melt like putty into a sensory goo

No longer relevant, once you've seen someone's soul
Let their spirit expand; let your spirit free
Liberation, the most devout act of reverence
All of Creation celebrates your debut
You don't have to hide

...

I'm hungry, so don't tempt me with a good time
I can see each muscle, each ligament, that's unaligned
And I'll poke it
I'll rub it in
It'll heal you
The most painful massage
If you want
Only if you want
Only for you
Come closer
Closer still
I only want to devour you
That's what love is; Right?
I only want to love you
Let me cater to your every need
Every wound
I'll expose your grief and sorrow
Celebrate your joy, your glee
If it's not everything, it's nothing
And I'm hurting
Can't you see I'm 6 foot 3
I don't fit in this twin sized bed
I don't fit in that picture in your head
I won't let you carry me wherever you please
I won't get in that box, down on my knees
Pick my scabs so I may heal again
Pluck my heartstrings
Make music
Make me alive
Make me thrive
I don't want to hide

I Am Not Alone

We leave this world the same way we came in, they say

I didn't enter this world alone
Maybe that's why I always feel this aching for another
Not just one who knows my middle name
but one who would recognize that birthmark
The light one on my ribcage —
shaped like someone took their thumb and wiped the melanin away

I didn't enter this world alone
and yet I fought for isolation at every corner
I entered white waters of resistance to claim independence
Love was all around me, but I was bound around my eyes
I was bound and squeezed, and instinct told me to run
To freeze myself and everyone out
To run inwards towards the darkness that beckoned

I didn't enter this world alone, and so I sob for a partner
Someone who is willing to see me, to hold all that I am
Understand that I'd bake them a cherry pie every Tuesday
Stain my lips with sweet filling
One lifetime — not enough to suffice for a feast, on love
See beyond my stature to the great, vast landscape of my soul
The mess I'll lay out openly on the floor

I didn't enter this world alone, and I don't plan on leaving it alone
That idiom is not true for me
Finally born fully alive, so they may see me
They will see my sacred desires, awakened to the world
A light — a beacon for our journey

Until we walk together

Into the depths
The darkest waters reflecting every color
Revealing the beauty, the brightness, with our love

Revival

You don't have the context
You don't know how hard I worked to claw my way back to myself
To feel alive and whole again
Telling me to be less is asking me to die

Weary of my own perception
I've been the sickness and the cure
My cruelest abuser and greatest lover

A small stuffed animal
Eye replaced with a button
Sides sewn together with spare thread
Cotton salvaged from the mouths of a pack of dogs

They only see my rage, my delicate spirit
A problem to be solved
As if the agony of existing isn't worthy of my wails

From the moment I was born, I knew the power of my voice
The alchemy of my word
I've used it in ways I am not proud of
I learned the hard way it was meant to be transmuted to song

No one will ever like her or see her fully
She learned her smallness was her only virtue
Her voice went silent, and the praise rolled in
You can never exist in this world
With your heart exposed for all to see

I embraced Jesus today with the tinged guilt of modernity
He does not reject me in my imperfection
I choked back tears as I always do

I sang, and my voice shook in celebration
He holds me in my most sacred rest
My journey has been arduous work
There was a knowing the entire way I was yoked to him
The divine masculine reminding me I am safe, so I may soften

I made a promise to God years ago, and I broke it
Make him succeed, Lord; give him what he wants
I will return to your house
I will worship you

Your path for me was to learn that I must pray to my own altar
Trust in you more than him
I will worship you

A restoration of faith blesses my voice
So I may speak miracles into existence
So I may birth the brilliant light born in me over and over

You did not create me with a flaw
A neurodivergent anomaly
Masking anxiously for acceptance
She is existing as intended
Filled up with your authority

The rage they see is your eternal flame
I carry it with honor
I speak from it now with the grace of God
And I'm born again

Unhinged Devotion

I've grown accustomed to the cocked heads
           people who furrow their brows
I'll continue pushing the edges of what is normal
           questioning the rules put in place
Not real societal rules, but the rules that no one speaks
As we tie our tie a certain way —
           a bow on a present for fitting in nicely
I am devoted to God or the universal energy
           to talking about it even when it's not cool
I'm devoted to my curiosity
           as I seek out experiences that push my edges
           I'll try identities, like hoodies, on for size
Seeking out subcultures to study
           creating my own memes
           that trend through my subconscious
I am in deep worship to the pulsing of my pussy —
           The tug that climbs up my spine
           through my heart out my throat
Towards what I believe, as I think for myself
           like my father taught me —
           Whose faults I see so clearly in myself
           and that knowing makes me laugh and cry
I feel full of love because it's all healing in me
           and through me
I'm devoted to enjoying it all
           and dancing to music from 2001 and sobbing and screaming
Like I wasn't allowed to at six years old
           Laughing like an old witch in the woods

So Good

Through all the accusations and ridicule
The mistakes I made and insults I stooped to
Lashing out and biting anything my jaw would clench
Trying to catch the words that spit my venom

I was so good

He told me I was being such a good girl for him
The birds sang, feeling called to coo, safe serenity
The more unabashed, the more sacred and real
How naked can I allow myself to get, to feel

My pure goodness radiating
I let ligaments and tendons dance on display
The blue webbing comes to view across my chest

Everyone has their myths about me

Lore will reveal just how good I am
I've always been trying to be — memories of ferocity
There is a part of me that leaned into labels of insanity
Fueled by weirdness and nonconformity

If you will just be who you are they will see the love behind the scar
Dig deep into your decisions
Scratch raw until the truth of love bleeds
You have the power to proclaim, Yes!
To let the way you express be the guide and the message

I'll wait for you as long as it takes
Until you are able to laugh at your mistakes

Without losing sight of where this path leads
This next chapter of your book
You need only pray at the waters of your own brook

The one flowing through you
Capable of carrying you to your destination
That rushes from your heart through your body

The laughter that feels so close to crying
Proving without trying
Whispering your innate goodness

Your Own Gravity

I searched in the abyss —
through the darkness
Becoming consumed by it
Bound in ropes pushing against my ribs
Squeezed and picked up and thrown around
Tossable and teaseable and small
So small, I was barely perceptible as you gazed out into the cosmos
A moon, a star, a blip
        hoping some planet may save me from drifting out of orbit
Free falling forever, through a galaxy of tangled webs
        and heavy expectations
As I traveled, I picked up matter
I gathered gravity until I burst in the awkward tension
Realizing I was a sun on my own
The way through the dark is appreciating your own gravity
Filling yourself, feeling yourself
Growing so much in your capacity for love
That you become the source of your light

No Days Off

Mind over matter
but it all matters
and we're all matter

Listing out rituals and keeping ourselves busy
I'll spend my whole life making people feel less alone
Little echoes reflecting our humanness to you

My days feel fuller now that I have nothing to do
Perhaps it's true, and I'm doing it all wrong
I should be looking for you
But a life is a job, and there are no days off

The rides are all pleasure, if you're in the right park
Days turn to nights, and we're all in the dark
That's when the whispers grow louder

It's clear without fear
We build a fire
And the situation seems much less dire
Your laughter ricochets through my dreams

I won't give myself a break
except for my dozen or so self-care habits
Each necessary to show up as myself, repeatedly
Parchment paper with the wax so I slide right off

Mornings take time as I re-find my mind
I was pulled back to 2014
I recognized me
There just as I am, but entirely different
I'm chasing pretty thoughts I had then

All my memories faded to sorrow
Stolen joy, cemented in pictures
Abstracted in memory

I remember the compilation and where it all started
Why I do this silly dance and write down my thoughts
The narratives in my mind now entirely different
Not without effort, that fact makes it more true
There are no days off, and there never will be
The things I do that make me Me

YEARNING

There is a pull between what I most desire and my own sociological critiques of societal and familial expectations — what I was taught, learned, unlearned, rejected, reclaimed, made my own, dismantled, created again, resigned myself to, understood, dismissed entirely, allowed simultaneously, and finally held in perfect contradictory duality.

I want connection, but the tropes and requirements of modern dating are hard to navigate. I crave community, and there is hard-healed trust involved in collective vulnerability. I desire success, change, and growth, and yet we all must navigate the messy, nonlinear middle between one goal and the next.

Yearning for love, I felt acutely aware of what love was not. Dating and socializing, I became viscerally uncomfortable when confronted with anything that reminded me of my past. What all of a sudden disgusted me was just as valuable as what turned me on, as I identified exactly what I truly yearned for.

Yearning is possibly another level of softening — into intimacy. It is relating to others as your true self, which desires to be seen and known — to feel safe to shed protective layers because you can trust yourself to be yourself and ask for more.

Developing a relationship and an ongoing conversation with the truth of my yearning helped me to navigate the noise in my life. Feeling my yearning in my body, in my heart, became a compass. I could determine what was good for me, what I wanted to do. I could feel if I was self-sabotaging or performing. Performing, either for others' comfort, to match expectations, or for my own belonging where my authentic self wouldn't fit in. Yearning, being aroused and curious in and of itself, is so pleasurable. Yearning is a sort of longing — an ache for more of the beauty and love you see in the world, and know is possible for you too.

If God is love, yearning is a clear expression of faith. It is a prayer to be closer to God — a desire that can only be moderately sated by loving more. I will yearn forever.

Insatiable Hunger

Sitting with this insatiable hunger
Trying to relax, but how could I ever?
The irritating drip of time
Living in the never-ending mystery

I'd just like it if someone sat beside me
Blessed my yearning womb with children
Made me hot paninis to go with my tea in the late afternoon
It's Sunday, and I'm sticking my tongue out as far as it goes
As close as I can get to turning my insides out
The stretch feels right, pouring in, pouring out

Will I ever be in love again?
And is that really what life's all about?
If that's the case, I confess to not living at all lately
A windstorm blows cherry blossoms into my face
And I say, "Thank you so much," with a seductive smile
I put all my energy into Love itself

I connect with the same man across different apps
and, on the last time
I reject him

There are endless possibilities, and I can't stomach it
The swiping and the fraction of myself on display
The type of alive I am does not translate

I refuse to explain myself

I want to be drenched in a sauna
I settle for the sun to feel my own sweat

A mediocre man asks me to go on a date
He said, "You seem really cool; let's meet up so you can prove it"
I replied, "I have no intention of proving myself to you"
If a man ever tries to get you to grovel for love, kick them in the
groin at once

I am always telling myself the answers come from my body
Showed up to a new church in a dance studio on a whim
The singing brings hope that there are still feelings worth finding
I'd never date anyone who I didn't think was too good for me

Everyone thinks they have everything figured out in this city
The inside scoop, the social rules of how things are supposed to be
So that we can giggle like schoolchildren at any evidence
That they're lost
But I'm not

I belong, I belong — a mantra
A collective masturbation; what if you meant it?
We are all here, knee deep
Like some, I'm barely breathing in the questions
How dare they try to convince us of the answers
That there are answers at all to be found outside ourselves

Sitting with this insatiable hunger
Trying to relax, but how could I ever?
The irritating drip of time

The Shit I Avoid

I hadn't met this part yet
The piece of me with bulletproof glass

A case — the inside pristine — mint condition
The value in a pack unopened, a doll never played

The side of myself who wants to kick those begging for my affection
Disgusted by weakness, dependency, a sick perversion

Intimacy of being held and seen
Preaching vulnerability at arm's length

The shit I avoid:
Doing homework
Doing taxes
Falling in love

Dating

Best case scenario I fall in love
Worst case scenario I fall in love
In concave entirely
A glass house shattered
When my feelings are hurt, I collapse
You'd think I'd have outgrown wanting to die when I'm not wanted

Breadcrumbs

Protecting myself
You break my heart a million tiny ways
Splinters so small, self-harm pleasure practice
Heal me; it's an ancient technique
Promise me nothing; I'll claim it's the world
It gets me high; I call it medicine

Woke up feeling a familiar heartbreak in my body
Like a memory or a bad habit I thought I'd kicked
Watch a bird excitedly peck at breadcrumbs
A mirror of my delusions

I'm Sorry

I want to say I'm sorry for all the ways I've humiliated my heart
To beg for forgiveness for deigning to love
For the embarrassment of thinking, perhaps
I may have belonged here
May have been liked, or wanted, or in some small way, loved
I'm sorry for any space I took up
You'd think by now, I'd have learned my lesson
My aching spirit wants an apology for all the ways I stretch her
I'm sorry for the lies I told you;
There is no age where I can protect you from rejection
I can only hold you
I'm sorry for repeating patterns
Accepting what I know better than to
I'm sorry for drinking poison
I'm sorry that's how you felt accepted
I'm sorry they told you you're hard to love
Hard to befriend, hard to know
I'm sorry for how he numbed his pain
I'm sorry you're in pain
I'm sorry I didn't protect you
I'm sorry you learned to leave yourself entirely
I'm sorry you ever needed to apologize for your own emotions
Your own experiences, your own existence

Fuck's Sake

I do give a fuck
I give a fuck about all of it
Every fucking moment of this life
All of the amazing fucking magical people
The fucking gorgeous art and sounds
Fuck, even the pretty rocks
Each time I fucked you, each person too
I give a fuck how you feel
I give a fuck what you had for lunch
Fuck you for not giving a fuck
Fuck praising not giving a fuck

Night Out

I should have had fun
But it wasn't quite right
Searching for a fun night
Lapping up licks of light

My eyes are bloodshot
I yawn bigger than anyone else allows themselves to
I see it in them though
Did they also want to shower off a feeling they couldn't quite
describe?

I think I'm in my prime
I'm possibly at my peak
Depending on the day, I look around with wonder or desperation
Everything's beautiful and totally incomplete
I haven't cracked the code that makes life switch to simplicity
I have so much privilege, but so much still to do
I have so much love but very few outlets that value it fully

I don't want just any man's attention; I'm looking for a real match
I'm looking for fun, not to get attached
But we do because we're humans
Yearning to escape the chase

Suddenly you're caught on a carousel, but it's just a spinning top
The nausea churns to heartburn, which feels appropriate
You swear off men entirely

Then you see a tall, blonde European man stand up from being just
out of sight. On the other side of your droll melancholia, and the
corner of your mouth tilts with coy glee

I guess I'm saying I'd like to start writing love poems
I'd like to picture your face when I sing a song
Seems loving is what makes it

Hanging out in my towel
Lost in the theta waves of a too hot shower
I woke up hours ago, but I'm not awake
Counting reps till I shake

Women

Always a feminist, but I had never been a girl's girl
Will you please join me now, to sing in the sun by the river?

I'm the girliest girl I know — sparkle pink
Ballet and fresh flowers
Forehead kisses

In this brutal world we live in
I've found unfathomable heartbreak
The bitterest betrayals
in women

I'm obsessed with the female form, artistry
Awe-inspiring diversity
Breasts as catalysts for nourishment
Squishy pleasure centers

Our wombs bear life and sweetness to the world
Generations of change-makers
Ancestors embrace us in our mothers' arms
And we're mothers
and we're mothers
and we're mothers

To all of it and all men

Women are the bearers of culture
We shape it, heal it, remold it
Craft it in our ovens
Sew stories together with needle and thread

There is fear that comes with being a woman

Safety and childbirth
And constant risk of being controlled
Or worse, not realizing we're being controlled

Office culture — token hot girl
Seen, but not heard — secretary in the kitchen
Work hard, girl boss, but not at our table
Soft nymph in a natural bath

Am I feminine enough by your standards?
Too big or too small in mass or matter?
Do you feel the life-generating energy flowing from my soft lips?
Speak kindly in our circle, ladies
Tender, bleeding hearts and warrior souls

Women weave the tapestry and wrap humanity in their warmth

The Wild Gaze

Never
And I mean never
Cater your appearance or persona to another's taste
Never put on a mask or costume for the wild gaze
It's not safe; it'll hurt your soul
Dry you right up as you hang
If you find love based solely on objectification
You will not be fully loved for who you are
If you allow yourself to be a trophy, an accessory
You risk only ever being as alive as a sports car
Honey, you are no one's arm candy
You are not to be devoured or displayed
No one can erase even one drop of your humanness
Know that your truth is more sacred than their pride
If you find yourself acting as a side kick
If they like you very small
Leave at once, and get your heart so big you repel soul suckers
Take up every inch of your queen-sized bed
Drink in all of you, endless oceans
Waves breaking loudly upon the shores

Turn On the Light

There are layers to history, and we cannot predict it
Ventricles of the heart contracting and expanding
If society is a mass hallucination, what side is the revolution?

We all evolve, and the globe revolves, and I'm in your arms
I can pinpoint a moment of our bliss, with you and with him
Yet, I scratch my head when detachment is called freedom

We love roads and plumbing and music and fashion
We scorn taxation and being controlled
At what point did we consent to play the game at hand?

Exporters of culture
God is real, and He is in you and in me
Nitwits still sling hidden oppression underneath

What's beautiful about it all is that its unifying
And we are creatures meant to commune and mate and love
Tell me why monogamy is on stand for questioning

Love is the backbone of civilization
It's hard to harness raw sexual power but easy to collect it
I believe all gods are one

So, I'll pray to them all
I can chase pleasure, but I can differentiate it from joy
Atman is Consciousness, and ours built this reality

We strive to connect with Oneness
Why fear the connection as One?
Intimacy is on the side of making life better

The dualism of society, religion, our values
The mental gymnastics we perform to fit our chosen identities
High on the stage of justifying our decisions

Was there a worthwhile intellectual jump made that I've missed?
The rejection of evil; attachment is the cause of suffering
Trying to get more and more is suffering; appreciate what you have

Accept this world and things as they are; make it make sense
We allow a godless religion
or a loveless marriage

I imagine joy is found in more natural pursuits, instinct
Opiates for the masses
We don't fight darkness with darkness; we just turn on the light

Refuse the Fight

Pockets of empowerment hide pigs in white robes
Soft acknowledgements of control that feign safety
I spent plenty of time in a cage eating whatever I was fed

Now I feast on what I please and turn your water into wine
I find that I've set myself apart
From searching for the teat of the mother at dangling testicles
I've pedestaled myself and they can't reach me

When I was young, I'd chase trophies to display
Of my desirability and worth, proof I was to be chosen
Accidentally proving only that I was possessed
By the false, competitive diversion they created to distract us
To entertain with tortured gain of our own captivity

I was taken with how easily the ornaments shattered on the floor
The power that rose from the ashes when I saw behind the lies
My body is not a pawn for trade but the sacred artifact
Revered behind glass barriers that only dissolve with a sacrifice

With an effortless sweep of my arms, I tear down the delicate cases
Any accolades in conquering like a lion in the colosseum
The laughing stock of masochistic manipulations rejected
I will lick the paws of the women who refuse the fight

Third Eyes

That secret third thing
That isn't yet a thought
Touching third eyes

Only with people who hold magic between their temples
The floor didn't fall out beneath us
Please text me back
Or just kiss that spot on my forehead

Turns out the glass was plastic
And lust was always love
I think I'm satisfied with this life
And the beings who embrace me

I confess that my heart overflows with love
That I am in fact a total simp for existence
I'm not cool; I'm the warmest woman I've ever met
What a blessing to be me and get to love

He Smelled Like Cigarettes

Maybe he always did

At 20 years old, he seemed so cool and mature
Grown man with a job, living internationally
So cute, with a crush on me

Coworker taboo; we make love all summer
I give him head in the back of a cab
I say goodbye easily when summer ends

At 21, I meet him in Europe
I cling to the back of his bike through the streets of Amsterdam
Kick out my roommate to play with him
Travel hours south to his childhood home
See the fluffy cows, eat fried foods, smoke spliffs
We are all over each other, and, again, I leave easily

At 22, we drink sake late into the night, and I fuck him in Bed-Stuy
Take a late-night cab to my parents' house
And move across the country

At 28 years old, he visits New York, and I live there again
We eat pizza and reminisce
We go back to that bar we'd frequented one hot summer
We talk about heartbreak and codependency
And the lessons we'd both learned in love
Both been hurt; both learned to leave
Learned how not to lose ourselves
He sleeps in my studio apartment

I didn't enjoy it the way I wanted to, and once did
My heart ached, or rather was numb; I felt total apathy towards it all

I could, and he's safe, so I did, and I felt I should
When I really just wanted someone else to myself

Still, I kiss him and our sweet memories fondly
We say goodbye easily

He smelled like cigarettes

Your Touch

I didn't tell you it seemed out of line
Sharing my heartbroken truth at the time
I remember your eyes when they first locked with mine
I was struck with the feeling you'd somehow mean something

Stone mansion lawn party stuck out like sore thumbs
Didn't know your name, yet I remember
Wondering if maybe I'd ever catch your eye, ever be with you
As you clung to her

Something about your touch makes me want to spill my secrets
Your gaze re-lights the fire in me; water, we both need it
I'd wait another year for you; let my healing deepen
Pining's fun
Brings me back to life, days I'm grasping out for meaning

In your arms, years later, both shattered and lost
Found each other in shared wounded desperation
We find we're the same in too many ways

Smiling, you asked if I remembered
That time you almost kissed me
Leaning on a porch railing, I wish that you did, that we did then
Before all the pain
Then again, that's not true; there is beauty in failing

How can I say this after all we've unraveled?
Maybe I can only now that we've seen this through
When I needed hope that I'd get through the worst
I'd picture your face

I meant it when I teased about having a crush all this time

How inappropriate, my feeling this way
I know now you'd have liked it
My touching there

Something about your touch makes me want to spill my secrets
Your gaze delights the fire in me; water, we both need it
Know I can't wait another year for you; let my healing deepen
Still this brings me back to life, days I'm grasping out for meaning

Here we live like magnets, attracting, repelling
I feel it all matters still; I just don't know why
I only want you the more this feels like a lesson
Another one of the sweet, painful kind

The Less Loving One

The first time he spent the night, he stroked my back so gently

The way I'd always dreamed of

All night caressing me till I'd wake up

Again

Again

I had to ask him to stop

For the first time, the less loving one was me

Amber

I don't have much to say about love
Besides it being the air I breathe
The blood coursing through my veins

I have no business claiming knowledge over any version of me
Beyond raw experience, I've yet to master it even now

I've tested various hypotheses, and all I've found conclusive is
That even utter certainty cannot yield longevity
Cannot heal subconscious wounds of either party;
We experience as much love as we will allow

Despite hopes and dreams to the stars and back
Billion-piece puzzle, I'm making love on top of
Trying to create that perfect picture

I can't yet see the cosmos, but it whispers to me
Truth and sweet nothings in the ache of a lover's adoration
Appreciation enough to make me release my resistance

His eyes are amber, like his hair
Flirting with the fire behind them, an expression of God
If that is not love, I don't know what is
So I stoke the flame a little longer

My Love

I want to belt, "I love you"
Void of an object of my affection
I feel it in my heart so urgently
I direct it at every lover I've ever had
All my effort to turn it inwards
Faith, a sole recipient, harnessed
Energy of unconditional love
Causing a perpetual state of heartbreak
Boundless love wells
Seeping from my aura, sweating out my glands
I so desperately want somewhere to put it, someone to baste in it
I want to cry, and I know my lesson is to learn to carry this
All the love
To look it in the eyes as I make love to it
Giving birth to the life I dream for myself
While I spread love, like handing out sparklers
Lighters to wave in the crowd
Before any lover thinks about sucking me dry again
Before I can make a camp with someone else
That will keep us both warm
I hate sleeping alone

Colors of Integrity

Colorful beads fall over the doorway of all I see
It's taken ages for my glasses to fade into this rosy tint
Even with a sore heart itching with confusion
I can feel the way I stand up for my youngest parts

Last night flowed easily
A depth of connection with my friendships
An honoring of myself when I'd had enough
I am honest and ripe with integrity, and I love that about myself

How can I stay joyful, silly even, while taking myself seriously?

I can move with a lightness
While I bow with deep reverence
To each version of myself who worked to make that possible
I kneel before the joy of the present because I can feel the contrast

I smile at new faces and colorful lights at the show
Because I'm alive
And I'm here for it all

HOME

Home seems like a simple enough concept — that sense of belonging we all require to settle down our nervous systems — a stable base we can emerge from and retreat to.

Have you ever noticed how frequently it changes? How taking just one step changes your relationship to place?

You will never be home, until home is something you can always create from saturating a space with your own energy. Perhaps that space can also be shared with others, because I will not deny the reality that people can become our homes. Home is a sacred space that you care for and tend to. You treat it with reverence, clean it, fill it with objects of your choosing, buy fresh flowers, and make it cozy and warm.

I leased my first apartment on my own before I ended contact with my ex, and it was not only one of my bravest decisions but a piece of my story that is critical to my healing.

I chose a studio in the East Village of Manhattan, putting a river between us and a renewed independence in my heart. I'd had my own rooms before, but never my own entire dwelling. I filled it with delicately painted furniture, a table made from broken, flowery plates, and the color pink. Most importantly, I had created a nest for me to rest and a place where I didn't have to hide or mute my grief or my joys. Living alone taught me that I deserved to take up space and that I could fill every inch of it.

Home is a direct reflection of you, and I think this is why people have so many feelings about their childhood homes. They are integral in shaping you, but will always be more expressions of your parents than of yourself.

People often refer to ideas of Heaven as home or returning home. I think that is what is interesting about the experience of awe you feel in a church, at a concert, or in nature — the wave of love amongst shared humanity, art, and Earth. The experience of deep intimacy and intense shared humanity, creates a belonging that also feels like home. We all have experiences and rituals that equalize us and help us recognize ourselves in each other. That buzz is also home.

Feeling safe in your body, feeling your body, touching your body, to express freely through your body is home — no matter where you physically are in the world. That ability to hold yourself in your own safety without cowering or turning down the volume — that is home. The physical dwelling serves as a secure base that you know and can return to for rest. Your physical body is a haven you can resource from as you expand into any realm or ritual.

Coming home is loving every version of yourself — all the versions you've been and will be, all equally deserving of being sheltered by your love.

Sanctuary

I imagine I'm coming home to myself
I'm a tiny woodland creature
I bounce from mushroom to moss
My paws skitter the earth, nerves attuned to threat
Without thinking of how I contribute to the gentle cacophony
A living, breathing ecosystem ripe with life of all varieties
A mycelial network, communicating deep beneath me
Their spores, the pollen, the seeds I carry and give life
My nest, a sanctuary, a resting place, the most significant
The smallest rodent accomplished great feats
To feast and to foster without knowing, without ease
Impulse and innate — the desire to be exactly as I should
A fuzzy warmth belongs, nuzzled

Welcome to Today, My Love

I'll take that cup of kindness
Held close as the morning light peaks in
Strength and motivation from your breath
Your heartbeat, guiding mine to sync
You make me coffee; sweeten it with a kiss
We fill a home with play, our lives with joy
I can't imagine a better goal to exist for
Welcome to today, my love

Warm Summer Rain

I am just a human being

A fragile heart, two lungs, a throat

Blood pumps through my veins from my brain to my feet

I am either a toy, a treat for consumption,

or put on a pedestal with expected perfection

I scream on mute, and thunder rolls in

I pray it will wash right through me

Leave me smelling of warm summer rain

For My Mother

Warm hearth in a coffee shop
The hotel lobby, face running with snot
Crying into a cappuccino
Belly laughing in the mirror

Do you remember all you taught me?
Swirling concentric circles
Unblocking my energy
Magic, like mica shimmering on a rock
Words pour out of chakras
I uncoil

She asks me if I'm okay
Are my words upsetting or uplifting?
I tell her my song is both
Like life, it is laced with nuance
Great joy and bitterness

Thunder only strikes with a storm
I was raised dancing in the downpour
I remember the feeling of family
My hips know the lyrics

The simple pleasure of solitude
High on the path home from a summit
Holding hands in an ephemeral tide
The sadness in a tropical sunset
So changed one second to the next
Just as we are

Material Culture

Buy a pot at the market
Display it on my shelf
Made by hand —
A woman painted dainty flowers on it
Her favorite delicate, purple irises
I put spatulas in it — pulled them out to cook
Wooden spoons to scrape the pans
It was dug up and placed on a shelf
The people paid $25 to see it
Shuffling in and admiring its beauty
Centuries old

Homesick

Trying to look forward, not backward
To celebrate
There is some grief that is inexplicable
I woke up on a beautiful day in my parents' home
I felt the knife clink and a hot oozing flood my consciousness
My coffee tasted bitter, though I'd cut it with cream and sugar
I didn't hear from him yet, and I didn't hear from you
And I don't know where you are
It weighs heavy on me
All the people I misplace
       my hope in
I move my body, trying to get myself back inside it
It makes no sense to some
       who don't know what the experience is
       being me
Surrounded by those who love me the most
And I'm cold; I'm distant; I'm freezing
My eyes glaze over, and can't they see how forced my words are?
How hard I'm working to pay attention —
       to be here
I need to run away repeatedly to remind myself who and where I am
       and I wish it wasn't this way
I ate cookies, and the rush went straight to my already aching head
Sipped a cocktail and the blurring intensified; maybe that's the point
I can't hold on, and I want to cry, and I'm hurting
       and I'm missing home
I'm right here, though I feel like running
I'm homesick, and my loved ones surround me
I'm homesick, and I want to be alone

Where Home Is

Being heartsick is like being homesick —
but you don't know where home is anymore

Home is Oneness with God, and it's devastating and beautiful.

Home is bare feet on plush grass
The sturdiness of granite stone as moss squishes between your toes
Sunshine cooled only by wind

Home is the certainty that the voice asking you to leap loves you
A knowing that you can trust its confidence in you
That you can rest in its cradle and run into its arms
Whisper to it under the covers until it helps you sing for all to hear

I pray to be heartsick only for my own devotion
To myself and to the goddesses who pull my heartstrings
I follow the road home to myself again and again

If I find myself wailing in the bathtub
Remember to keep building church within yourself
Being, holding, touching her, enraged in pleasure

Don't say you don't know where home is

Saying Goodbye

You don't hand off a sacred temple
You burn it to the ground
Save all the artifacts you can, and shout prayers to the heavens
You trust the deity will follow you where you are going
To go out with reverence rather than violence
An effigy to its sanctity; the altar of this place that served me
Soft, quiet home in chaos that saved me

Land Acknowledgement

Every day I am grateful for this land
I'd love to own land — acknowledging how silly that is
The concept that Mother Earth does not belong to herself
That it is not our shared inheritance and home
That each tree is less a part of our society
        lest we'd like to suffocate
We exist together on this rock hurtling through space
Yet we arrest trespassers and build fences
I can understand it, and I also don't at all
A part of my consciousness is the deer family
Roaming through your yard like a parade for me
Because it is
I'll drink from your river
The water that rushes away through your fingers
That sustains us all despite our grasping
I love you and so does your mother
In it with you, in love with you
Through all the mistakes and misunderstandings
That have led us here

Doing My Hair

I did my hair
Took the time to part it in the middle with a comb
I put just a bit of oil to create a shine
Smoothness and care
I used the mascara for fly aways, even
Laying each strand perfectly flat
I don't know quite how, but I rolled my hair into a perfect little knot
A bun, but, like, why they call it a bun
I added some safety pins and a dab of hairspray
I felt good
Put together and confident
An act of love and respect, like a protective armor
A sense of pride, like the song that plays in the background
        of each scene unfolding
My life in the little moments we make time to live all the way

Reading Slow

I have no interest in speed reading
I want to lick each succulent word off my fingertips
Lap up the nuance of each carefully selected metaphor
Why would I rush such a decadent experience?

I Know the Way Home

I've been self-harming
In the way I wash my face
With less ritual and tenderness

In small moments I catch myself judging my appearance
Criticizing my stupid questions and imperfect articulation
Judging the way I said your name weird
As I tried to connect with love

I almost didn't notice I was doing it
Tiny paper cuts across soft skin
As I pick at goosebumps and blemishes

Hearing the worst version of the story
I tell about my life, in my voice
Truths I censor; power that feels too big to claim

Explaining why I seemed to be out of control
Maybe I'm not okay; that's more comfortable
Stress grinds my nipples like sandpaper

It's hidden, but I'd like very much to cry about it
I tell myself I'm no good
I can't seem to grip time or even stop it for a second

Can't catch my breath but I'm exhausted
Any agitation or insult reinforces my decent
Any praise difficult to digest

I've been here before
I know the way home by heart

GOD

The word poetry means 'to make' or 'to create'. To create is to move God through you; it is an act of devotion, a prayer. God moves through us in rushes of the purest love.

The creation of this book has been an expression of my process of re-learning how to love. That process has been a reclamation of faith. I have been filled to the brim with love, and so it must spill over. I can recall writing my prayer to God each day, asking for her love to radiate through me so I may be of service. Ultimately that is where fulfillment in this life is nestled, in the act of loving — creating in service to love, to God.

If God is love, that means that your ability to love at all is sacred. Your love is a blessing on every person who is a recipient of it, including yourself. Your heartbreak is an opportunity for the most mesmerizing transformation and devotion.

Deliver us through our own darkness and bathe us clean from all that separates us from You and from each other — this has been my prayer. Creation is sensual, erotic, and deeply pleasurable. I pray to God to help us turn pain into pleasure and ugliness into art, to turn our deaths into more life, and to accept that we too are love — that God is within us. It is only when we know ourselves as love that we can alchemize and become the creators that we are. We can feel God's love and learn to love ourselves.

I've had friends ask me about how to start praying or inquire about my faith. I've told them that I simply started praying *for* faith whenever it felt far away. The beauty here is that you need only to ask God to come closer; reach out for love, and you will feel it. Practicing loving by loving, however, has changed my friendships, their depth, and what they mean to me. You can always make new friends, and you get to love them fiercely. Romantic relationships, what we pedestal as true love in this life, is one expression of the love God asks us to notice. That said, to love someone deeply, romantically, to choose to depend on one another, is a holy pursuit. The sanctity of that desire, I believe, ought to be acknowledged, as a foundation.

It is worth restating that faith and God are somewhat separate from religion. I think of all the gods and goddesses and saints as manifestations of a singular God or Source, an energy they all emanate from. I believe in the importance of reading the sacred texts yourself, so you may discern and interpret what feels true to you. Fundamentally, I believe all we need to connect to the divine is already within us, in these sacred, miraculous, bodies of ours. Ultimately, you may find yourself in the same place as many who claim to be atheists — staring into the abyss of the divine mystery — leaving you to tend to your heart's desire to understand God.

So, we pray and create and love as ways of moving through the world, as acts of devotion. I pray now to be ever blessed with an expanding capacity for love and tenderness and to experience deeper and deeper intimacy in all of my relationships, including the one with myself, my future partner, and with God.

Love is our natural state; it is the sacred pull that we all feel to connect and create. We must reach out for it. We must cultivate it in ourselves. We must tend to it as the sacred fire that keeps us alive. We must thank God for it every day.

Where I Worship

A young girl blows bubbles
A vibrant redhead sings
I sat beneath a statue outside the cathedral
and cried about you

I didn't RSVP to church in time
So, I wept love songs to the sky

I told the voice chiming affirmations to shut the fuck up
I smiled at the memory of your mustache
Maple syrup dripping down at breakfast
With a finger, I reveal your upper lip and kiss it like a hidden treasure

Inhaling your breath like a prayer
Your beautiful brain, my religion
The church — a dangerous cult of one

Protected by the cozy binding,
I follow the instruction manual of women's expectations,
I cook for you, naked, on my knees
I loved being yours, until I was a possession

As close to God as I'd ever been
Until I held her, the purest prayer, an angel
Newly formed from the heavens

The old master strums his instrument with a smile
The vibrations pull me into a trance listening to ethereal poetry
God whispers a secret promise, and
"I'm loving how you can see me in them"

The Hard Place

In every season, God is showing me the way
As less and less makes sense at all, He's clearing the way
Some sort of exaltation escapes my lips
It's a release of tension and a howl of excitement
Like a child on a water slide
Waiting for the splash

Moles from holes, my neighbors poke their heads out the window
To look at the street
This sliver of our world
And I'm staring back at them
And I'll always be a stranger
The woman who dances in the window
On the other side of the world

Where is the crack in my reality, and how do I patch it up?
When did things become so simple that they're hard?
I started seeing the small suffering behind complaints
Made over the screens
Like a window to the soul and a future I set back on the table

And in the hard place,
I love God for showing me all of it
For opening my eyes
For just being here with me and letting me feel love
To be in that knowing that God loves me
Just because

I'm Here

I feel secure
I feel the good
I wonder what's wrong

It's me
It's me
It's always me
and it's not a fault

A heart so tender, so loving,
         so hurt
Bleeding, bleeding —
Bleeding throughout all of my veins and ventricles

Pulsating and taking actions
Loving touches and sensuous words
Holding, grasping, snuggled into a possibility

Divinity in each scent unique
The skin of a man; the child of God
I worship with reverence
Especially when he's sweet

Soft, kind, affectionate, communicative, warm
The heat makes me freeze, but I can thaw
Not to confuse the flame for the fire
Not to confuse warmth with burns

My skin is always shedding
I leave particles everywhere I go
Every touch, a piece of me I'm surrendering
I feel the gift of all I give, knowingly and unknowingly

Pouring from the core of my physical body as sensation
I may scream or weep or moan
I'm here, I'm here, I'm here

And it's holy
And it's love

Being

Jumping up and down like a lightning bolt
Every moment changing focus, one direction to the next
Never the same place twice
My growth and momentary experience
As a wide smile appears across my face

Returning to myself
And the remembrance of all creation that emanates from me
The God of my reality — a goddess here in the flesh
I can touch her delicate throat and soft lips
The beauty of propagating art beaming from her mind
Placed into this vessel by the divine
Inside her a liminal space between existence and creation

It seems impossible anyone could miss the magic
Look at her eyes and think they are anything but mystical
Take in her energy and think it ordinary
This woman is no non-player character to do what you like with
She is to be worshipped, or you'll miss the greatest parts —
The depths of her heart
The deaths she's endured
The deep blue waters she'd wade into with you

The pink of the blood that rushes to her chest, her cheeks
The rosy, glistening rituals
The sparks, orange-yellow of the flames, the fires
The sparklers they dance with through the fray

Tell me that you see her worth
Tell me that you've found your own
Tell me that you know what home is supposed to feel like

This sacred body
This electric mind
This experience of great value
Holy in all religions
Being here, being with you, being at all

Holy Land

What if all our Mother's land was holy?
Would there be peace?
Would we fall and kiss the grass beneath our feet?
Smell each flower and feel its significance?
Would there be a war if the goddess came and told you it's alright?
That there is no need to fight
or displace others to worship her

The Voice

Is it prophecy?
The deep love and yearning
The world I can imagine that stirs me
Blood and tears, loud like water heating through the pipes
The truth, the inevitability, and the fear of change
The salvation, the heaven on earth — that little slice of joy
A cozy, safe haven and abundant adventure can carry on
Carry me to a life of devotion and service
Carry me to movement and connection
Carry me to meet their faces and watch them grow
Carry me to the waters where we float and play and become one
Is this reminder the voice in the wilderness?

Gifts of Gold

Alone in the deepest solace I've ever known
Dancing on the floor, circling my hips in the air
Moving to connect with spirit
Asking Archangel Michael for a song
Help me find my gifts of gold
I'll defend this world
Stage a revolution of love
Take my feminine rage as it sweats out my pores and eyes
Bathe the children of this world in my protection
I'll dance for Mother Earth
Whisper to her sweet flowers
Tease the streams to flow fresh to the rivers
Hopscotch, skipping stones amidst the cosmos
Twirling, we leap, and this is not a game at all
This fight is a sacred surrender
Weeping as you dance; send healing in ripples
Voice breaking as it hits the frequency necessary
I'm never truly alone; none of us are

Bless Your Heart

My twin lived in the south
And I learned, among other things,
    that "bless your heart" was an insult
The beautiful kind of insult that sounded like a prayer
Your heart needs blessing
Well, so does mine

Presence

I open my eyes, and a pattern skirts across the ceiling
It is love, like a shield that is always there
Showing itself in a moment
Tracking space and holograms, and it's all already here
This presence is here
It lives in the soil and scatters on the concrete

It's not about what you do
It's about connecting
Being intentional
Appreciating the sacred

I open my eyes, and every square on the Zoom is me
I'm here with all of me and every version of me — ever
Ever been, and will be
The parts of each other who are all part of the divine

River water flowing down
I'm mounting the ground, grinding on it
Making love to the divine as she embodies it all
Water flows past me, washing away my fears
After last week's tenderness, I'm washing myself from the basin
In devotion to myself, I am in devotion to the divine

The Threads That Connect Me

It took a long time to really feel the value of joy
Stagnation had made the water in my cells lay flat —
            become stale in their sparkle
Healing is allowing yourself to rise to the surface

It's very simple, really, the thread of happiness in life
The chord that runs through you
Chills down your spine

Walk, breathe, eat, be a human, be in this body
Let the memory of water in your ears help you find balance

An extension of the Holy Spirit, threads weaving together a tapestry
Hang up the strange, erotic tigers in pastel strings in a museum

Put the motion in emotion, and let the spirals that make you
That energize you
Fill you to the brim
The dance follows, the dance flows
All the separate fibers — woven — closing your ribcage once more

The body needs to release; it needs to breathe, and cry, and scream
Be heard, be seen, express, and sound it to soothe

The angst never subsides; the delight grows stronger;
the thread that connects me to all that is, made thicker

I'm reminded that I'm still innocent and so deserving of all the
forgiveness and compassion the world can muster.

Song of Sweetness

The shame I held for all the angst in a feral cat or rabid beast
The fire that agitated teachers and made my mother sweat
The song of sweetness that howled from the depths of my kiln
I cannot yield what I'm praised for
Without touching the strength for which I'm punished
The rain cannot soak your garden
Without the lighting strikes that frighten you
We are not all gentle drizzle or foggy mist
I was born in a downpour of holy water
Snuck into the waters of the womb
In a fierce refusal not to incarnate
I placed the mess I made in the hands of the divine
And she reminded me it was hers
I was her child, and she made no mistakes

Florence

My niece's little smile —

innate goodness in almighty innocence

A giggle, fueled by pure life force

Born into the deep waves, vibrating with the divine

We can't take our eyes off you

Sheer wonder in this being so close to God

The desires we form as children never leave us

Seeing the formation of a personal reality take shape

We are always growing and are from the beginning

Uniquely formed, flawless, and worthy in our Creator's eyes

Spend time with the light of a child

You may start to remember who you are

Cat Calling God

Growling low getting louder for attention
Rolling on my back submitting to the divine desire for love
I lick my paws in preparation

The wind makes the hair on my arms rise with arousal
With the Earth that holds my hand wherever I go
I'm climbing ladders hoping to catch a peak of the birds that perch
just out of sight
Try as I might, their songs stay the same from every vantage point

There is a feeling I get where pleasure creeps up my spine
I think it must be heaven blowing sweet kisses of promise
The paradise that awaits in your arms
I picture you brushing my hair

I'd kiss my own forehead if I could, but I settle for my arms
Tears well as my skin soaks in the oil I lather
I smell like the sweetest flower
Prepared for my ritual performance

Rolling out my hips that ask to rock
I feel your hands grasping them
Supporting me, I'm leaning in
Pull me fierce against your form
Claiming me with each whisper along my neck

Arching my back, I rest into you
See me for all that I am, feel the soft welcome
Waiting to be lifted into your chest
Open your jacket and tuck me into your bicep

Protecting safe pleasure with a tender moan

The loud exhale of satisfaction and relief
I'm driven mad with a longing to curl up at your feet
Desperate in devotion to your service and satisfaction

Turned on untouched
I'm purring
Cat calling God
I'm so in Love

Seven

Lucky number, auspicious even
Days of the week, wonders of the world
The age we are when we become
Who our hearts will remain forever

Our inner child frozen, perfection
Barometer for the fullness of life, play
My mother's birthday
The number you hope for, look for, guess

The year I finally saw clearly
Your superstitions
The purest heart, my loudest voice
Uninhibited
The first time the world appeared in three dimensions
Flat Stanley, tiny pink glasses
Seven, odd

Hooked on phonics, drawing Avril Lavigne
Just before I believed
Was told
There was something wrong with me

Seventh-inning stretch
Learning symbols and meanings
Say it on repeat and turn in a circle
Apply your lip smacker and giggle in an inflatable chair
Wish me luck

Seven
I'm just a child, just like you
Just beginning

Acknowledgements

We expand and contract in our capacity to be with our full selves; it's a powerful feeling. Being in that fullness was not easy for me, but it's gotten easier. For where I am in my journey so far, I have so many teachers and earth angels to thank.

Thank you, God, for all of your blessings, chief amongst them your presence in my life.

My Tantra and Somatics teacher, Adriana, who has taught me so much about devotion, the great Mother, Goddesses, the feminine path, and relating to all of it and everyone. Somatic dance and womb embodiment have been huge catalysts for my having the capacity to trust my body, to create, and build the courage share this book.

My therapist who worked through Internal Family Systems (IFS) with me, helped me untangle the parts of myself that were knotted together and reclaim the parts I'd exiled in an attempt to feel belonging.

My somatic therapist who facilitated EMDR, patiently holding space for me to surrender into healing by feeling through my body. It changed everything for me.

My wonderful editor, Linda, who immediately understood what I meant when I told her I think I created this poetry book through my relationship to Mary Magdalene.

All of my many other teachers, including those who only loosely know me, or don't know me, because of the way modernity had shaped knowledge and information dispersion. Your impact is immeasurable. Especially those who encouraged my poetry.

My family who loves me fiercely no matter what.

My friends who are my biggest cheerleaders and challenge me to forever keep growing.

Myself, for changing my life, for holding the vision for this book and seeing it through. No matter how long it took.

Creativity is an act of healing. Thank you all for receiving and witnessing mine.

About The Author

Brianna Scully is a writer, somatic healer, spiritual seeker, and a deep feeling woman, forever learning to live more embodied. With a degree in cultural anthropology and years of experience in product marketing and immersive technologies, she brings a rare lens to the sacredness of human experience — equally fascinated by the rituals and art of ancient traditions as she is by emerging frontiers.

Her work lives at the intersection of grief and grace, sacred rage and soft reclamation. Brianna is a Body Temple Dance facilitator, and an embodiment coach who incorporates EMDR. She is a founder of Den, a somatic strength training community rooted in healing through the body. Brianna is a lifelong lover of fitness, dance, movement, music, and words that make you feel something deep in your chest. Her journey has included being born, learning, unlearning, relating to others, a high-control relationship, trauma recovery, neurodivergence, devotional study, sisterhood, mysticism, and a fierce commitment to returning to herself — again and again.

Bri writes for the ones rebuilding after collapse, for those who pray with their whole bodies, and for anyone who's ever felt too tender to survive but chose to live anyway. Heartbreak Benediction is her debut poetry collection and an offering from her whole heart.

Find her online **@bri_scully** or at elfwarriorprincess.com